THE AMERICAN MATCH

THE OFFICIAL WORLD LEAGUE YEARBOOK 1992

THE AMERICAN
MATCH

THE OFFICIAL
WORLD
LEAGUE
YEARBOOK 1992

DAVID TOSSELL

 Budweiser B⬛XTREE LLVN/π

DAVID TOSSELL

DAVID TOSSELL is assistant sports editor and American football correspondent of the *Today* newspaper. One of the country's leading gridiron writers, he has covered Super Bowls, American Bowls and followed the London Monarchs back and forth across the Atlantic, as well as being a former player himself for the Windsor Monarchs and Slough Silverbacks. He celebrates his thirty-first birthday on the opening day of the 1992 World League season.

First published in 1992 by
Boxtree Limited
36 Tavistock Street
London WC2E 7PB

1 3 5 7 9 10 8 6 4 2

Text © TM & C 1992 World League
Photographs © Dave Shopland Sports Photography 1992
Photograph on page 83 © Bob Straus 1991

Designed and edited by
Anness Publishing Ltd
Boundary Row Studios
1/7 Boundary Row
London SE1 8HP

Colour reproduction in Hong Kong by Fotographics
Typeset by Central Southern Typesetters, Eastbourne
Printed and bound in Great Britain by Richard Clay Ltd,
Bungay, Suffolk

A CIP catalogue record for this book is available from the British Library.

ISBN 1-85283-180-4

CONTENTS

1
THE HISTORY
OF THE WORLD LEAGUE

WHEN the World League kicks off its second season on March 21st, there will be a lot of people on both sides of the Atlantic who will be swallowing a second helping of humble pie. From the moment that the National Football League announced in early 1989 that they were studying the possibility of setting up an international spring league, the voices of the cynics could be heard. It will never happen, they said. Well, it happened. Even though the locations of some teams weren't announced until four months before the scheduled kick-off, and despite the players only being allocated to their clubs with a month to go, the 1991 World League season went ahead almost without a hitch. It culminated in a memorable evening at Wembley in June, when the London Monarchs became the first winners of the World Bowl.

For a few weeks, while competition went ahead in five different countries and two different continents, the cynics were silenced. Then, when the dust had settled on the first season, the cynics found their voices again as tales of poor American television ratings and heavy financial losses started to emerge. The owners of the NFL teams – 26 of whom formed the WLAF shareholders – decided to look closely at the question of whether the league was viable. They are going to shut it down, gloated the critics. But on October 23rd last year, the doubters were silenced again, perhaps for good this time. The World League announced that the owners of the NFL had given them their unanimous backing. With a three-year television deal with ABC TV and USA Network in place and buoyed by the magnificent response to the league in Europe, the NFL approved a three-year financial package to help the World League build on the successes of its first season. With all 28 NFL teams now on board as shareholders, plans were announced to expand the league from its current 10 teams to 12 in 1993 and 14 in 1994. Hardly the scenario the league's knockers had envisaged.

The key element in the equation was undoubtedly the World League's success in clinching an extension to their original two-year deal with ABC TV. Indeed, it had been at the instigation of two American television networks that the NFL had begun their research into the formation of the World League. Following the success of the NFL's American Bowl series of games held annually in London and other foreign cities – and the continued growth of interest in the NFL around the globe – a decision was quickly reached that the time was right for overseas expansion of America's favourite sport. Former Dallas Cowboys chairman Tex Schramm was the man chosen by the NFL to head the new league and one of the first people appointed to serve under Schramm was a former Cowboys executive, Billy Hicks. By the time the World League was ready to confirm the London Monarchs as their third European team 18 months later, Hicks, by then the WLAF's European coordinator, was considered the ideal man for the job of general manager of what was probably the league's key franchise.

Hicks set about the task of putting together an administrative staff at the team's new home, Wembley Stadium. Then came the job of finding a head coach. As soon as Hicks interviewed Larry Kennan, the offensive coordinator of the Indianapolis Colts and winner of a Super Bowl ring while an

● **London Monarchs running back Judd Garrett (22), the league's leading receiver in 1991, takes on the New York-New Jersey Knights.**

assistant coach at the Los Angeles Raiders, Hicks knew he had found the Monarchs' first head coach. Together, the two men planned their strategy in the league's first draft and, on what Hicks admits was an emotional occasion, the Monarchs finally took the field on the first day of their training camp in Orlando, Florida. Four weeks later the Monarchs' British kicker Phil Alexander, one of four non-American players assigned to each team under the league's Operation Discovery scheme, kicked off the first World League game in Frankfurt – and the rest is history. They said it would never happen, and it did. They said it would never happen for a second time, and on March 21st it will. The cynics had better get used to the idea – the World League of American Football is here to stay.

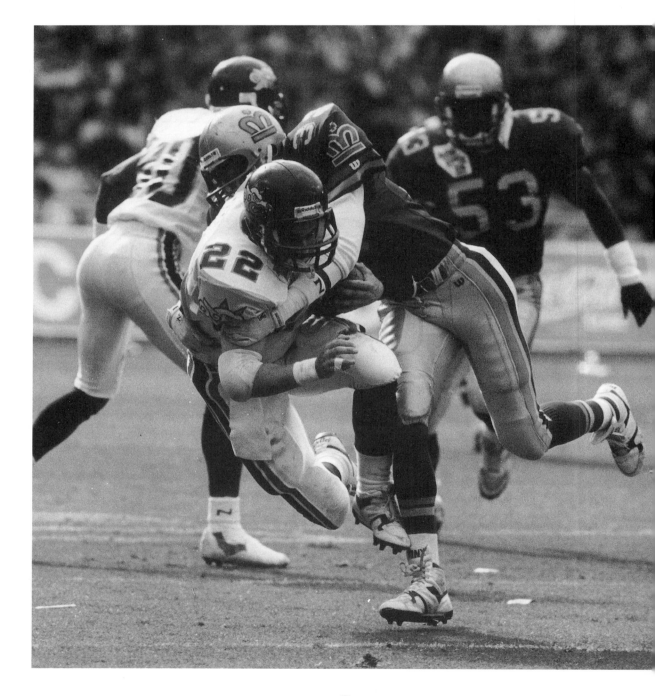

○ **Barcelona Dragons running back Jim Bell (22) is tackled by London Monarchs safety Dedrick Dodge (33) during the first World Bowl.**

WORLD LEAGUE

DIARY

○ **APRIL 18, 1989** Tex Schramm is appointed president of the World League and chief executive officer. He is assigned by the NFL to conduct a feasibility study into the proposed new league.

○ **JULY 1, 1989** The NFL announces a unanimous decision to go ahead with the World League and later names spring 1991 as the kick-off date.

○ **FEBRUARY 6, 1990** The World League announces a two-year deal with ABC TV, worth $24 million, to show live matches on Sunday afternoons.

○ **MARCH 10, 1990** The World League agrees a four-year cable television package with USA Network, worth a further $25 million.

○ **MARCH 15, 1990** Orlando, Florida, is awarded the first World League franchise.

○ **MAY 19, 1990** Barcelona, Spain, is the first European city to be awarded a World League team.

○ **AUGUST 3, 1990** London is confirmed as a World League franchise, with home games to be played at Wembley Stadium.

○ **OCTOBER 19, 1990** Mike Lynn, long-time general manager of the NFL's Minnesota Vikings, replaces Tex Schramm as president of the World League.

○ **NOVEMBER 14, 1990** The World League announces plans for its inaugural season, with 10 teams split into three divisions: North American West (Birmingham, San Antonio, Sacramento), North American East (New York-New Jersey, Orlando, Montreal, Raleigh-Durham) and European (London, Barcelona, Frankfurt).

○ **DECEMBER 6, 1990** London's team is officially given the name of the Monarchs, with Billy Hicks as general manager.

○ **FEBRUARY 4, 1991** Larry Kennan is appointed head coach of the London Monarchs.

○ **FEBRUARY 12, 1991** The World League's unique position-by-position player draft begins in Orlando.

○ **FEBRUARY 25, 1991** The London Monarchs open training camp in Orlando.

○ **MARCH 10, 1991** The Monarchs arrive in England and take up their headquarters at the United States International University, Bushey, Hertfordshire, where the players will live and practise for the next three months.

○ **MARCH 23, 1991** The World League season kicks off.

○ **JUNE 9, 1991** The Season ends as London Monarchs beat Barcelona Dragons 21–0 in first World Bowl at Wembley.

○ **OCTOBER 23, 1991** The NFL announces a three-year plan for backing the World League, which will expand to 14 teams by 1994. The league announces a new three-year television deal with ABC.

○ **FEBRUARY 4–5, 1992** Second World League draft takes place.

○ **MARCH 21, 1992** The second World League season kicks off.

9

2
THE 1991 SEASON IN REVIEW

WORLD LEAGUE president Mike Lynn touched down in a helicopter to present the official game ball, British kicker Phil Alexander booted it high into the cool spring air above Frankfurt's Waldstadion, and at last the moment league officials had prepared for and agonised over for two years had arrived. But by half-time of the WLAF's opening match all those elaborate plans and high hopes appeared in danger of disappearing down the Rhine.

League officials had spent many long hours convincing critics that their brand of football would be the real thing. Yet a stumbling, fumbling first 30 minutes did little to support their case. The jury of 23,169 fans suffered through a first quarter which featured only 41 yards of offense and highlighted the problems of putting teams together from scratch at only a month's notice. Monarchs quarterback John Witkowski, in particular, was a victim of the unfamiliarity of his offensive line. They allowed Frankfurt Galaxy nose tackle Chris Williams through to tackle running back Judd Garrett in the end zone for a safety – a suitably inauspicious way for the first World League points to be put on the board. Frankfurt took a 5–0 lead on Stephan Maslo's 25-yard field goal, but with the Monarchs able to apply pressure to Galaxy quarterback Mike Perez, the home side never threatened to break the pattern of defensive dominance which continued until midway through the second quarter. It was then that the Monarchs finally embarked upon a 13-play, 73-yard drive that looked as if it actually belonged in a game of pro football. London head coach Larry Kennan sent in David Smith at running back. Having helped move his team to the Galaxy 28-yard line, the fleet-footed Smith took advantage of superb blocking to race through a gaping hole in the Galaxy defensive line for the Monarchs' first touchdown.

Kennan's team began the second half with a new-found confidence. Dana Brinson returned the opening kick-off 47 yards and quarterback Stan

● **Frankfurt safety Mark ●eals (22) attempts to get ● grips with London ●unning back David Smith ●2).**

● **London Monarchs wide receiver Dana Brinson flips the ball away in celebration after scoring a touchdown.**

Gelbaugh, replacing the luckless Witkowski, enjoyed improved protection from his offensive line to set up Alexander's 25-yard field goal. The play which had league officials breathing heavy sighs of relief and the Monarchs sideline dancing with delight came with London in apparent trouble on their own four-yard line. Gelbaugh dropped back, eluded the Galaxy pass rush and launched a bomb downfield for receiver Jon Horton. Beating his defender, Horton pulled off a spectacular catch and raced past the celebrating Monarchs bench for a breathtaking touchdown. The World League had arrived. 'Jon's effort was outstanding,' said Kennan. 'And Stan threw the ball very well, right on the money'.

Kennan was soon rejoicing in an eight-yard scoring run by Brinson. Even a late Galaxy touchdown from Todd Young failed to take the gloss off his team's victory. 'I'm thrilled for everyone,' said Kennan. 'It's great to be here and be part of the first World League game and I'm really proud right now to be a London Monarch. I love our guys, they really rallied when we were behind.'

Quarterback Gelbaugh, who completed 10 of 16 passes for 189 yards, adopted an optimistic tone when asked about the future of the World League. 'As long as you get fan support like we did tonight, I don't see how you can lose.'

● The most dramatic game of the opening week was in Orlando, where San Antonio twice came from 14 points down, only to lose 35–34 when kicker Teddy Garcia missed an extra point attempt with less than two minutes remaining. Birmingham disappointed their 53,000 crowd by failing to score a touchdown in their 20–5 defeat against Montreal, while Sacramento's Paul Frazier clinched a 9–3 win against Raleigh-Durham with a one-yard touchdown. Barcelona's 19,223 rain-soaked fans saw their team score 19 points in the second quarter to beat New York-New Jersey 19–7.

W E E K	1	S T A R S

PASSING	★ Kerwin Bell (Orlando) 14 of 34 for 269 yards, 5TDs
RECEIVING	★ Jon Horton (London) 3 for 115 yards, 1TD
	★ Byron Williams (Orlando) 4 for 113 yards, 3TDs
	★ Kenny Bell (Birmingham) 10 for 93 yards
RUSHING	★ Elroy Harris (Montreal) 17 for 92 yards, 1TD
	★ David Smith (London) 18 for 87 yards, 1TD

RESULTS (*Away team first*): Sacramento Surge **10**, Birmingham Fire **17**; Raleigh-Durham Skyhawks **20**, Orlando Thunder **58**; New York-New Jersey Knights **18**, London Monarchs **22**; Frankfurt Galaxy **10**, San Antonio Riders **3**; Barcelona Dragons **34**, Montreal Machine **10**.

London Monarchs running back Judd Garrett is halted by Frankfurt Galaxy defensive back Joe Greenwood during the league's opening game.

Monarchs punter Greg Horne gets his kick away under pressure from the Knights at Wembley.

THE LONDON MONARCHS achieved the first of two main objectives from their opening home game at Wembley Stadium before a ball had even been kicked. An attendance of 46,952 was as large as even the most optimistic of team officials could have hoped for. By the end of a thrilling evening's entertainment, those fans had taken their new team instantly to heart and cheered them lustily to a 22–18 victory that was in the balance right up until the dying seconds.

Once again, the early signs were not good for the Monarchs. New York running back Eric Wilkerson galloped 74 yards on the Knights' opening drive, setting up a simple one-yard touchdown run for quarterback Jeff Graham. More trouble loomed when Knights kicker Barry Belli lined up a 27-yard field goal, but linebacker Rickey Williams slid inside his blocker to throw himself in the way of the kick.

Monarchs kicker Phil Alexander passed his first test of nerve in front of his home crowd by landing a 40-yard field goal. Thanks to their ability to penetrate a porous New York offensive line and a vital end zone interception from safety Dan Crossman, the London team kept the deficit down to only 7–3 at half-time. Knights coach Darrel 'Mouse' Davis would confess later, 'The turning point was when we threw the interception when we were going in for the touchdown just before half-time. Big plays normally win games and that was one right there.'

Quarterback Stan Gelbaugh, who had himself been intercepted three times in the first half, began to produce some big plays of his own after the interval. His 38-yard completion to Dana Brinson paved the way for David Smith to barge in from two yards. After Brinson left the field injured and Smith had been ejected, Gelbaugh lofted a sweet pass into

Knights quarterback
**Jeff Graham (9) is sacked
by Danny Lockett and
Virgil Robertson (55).**

the hands of receiver Andre Riley, who outpaced the Knights defense for a 62-yard score. London linebacker Danny Lockett's third sack left Belli lining up to punt from inside his own 10. Safety Dan Crossman broke through to block the kick and recover the loose ball for a touchdown, making the score 22–7. All the Monarchs had to do to win the game comfortably was control the ball and the clock.

It proved easier said than done. Wilkerson scored from seven yards and, following a successful two-point conversion, a fumble from Monarchs running back Jeff Alexander set up a Belli field goal which cut the gap to 22–18. It was left to Dedrick Dodge to save the day with two interceptions inside the final four minutes. The second came as Graham took a final shot at the end zone with 10 seconds left, prompting the crowd to break into a deafening

chorus of 'Land of Hope and Glory' as time ran out. The fans' contribution was recognised in the locker room by coach Larry Kennan, who said, 'The way the crowd got behind us made us feel even more part of the city. They were awesome.'

Orlando Thunder's prolific offense continued to roll along with a 58–20 thrashing of Raleigh-Durham. Quarterback Kerwin Bell, again named Player of the Week, guided Orlando to scores on the first six possessions. In Birmingham, John Miller's 99-yard interception return gave the Fire a 17–10 w against Sacramento, while a Mike Perez touchdown pass to Cedric Gordon was decisive in Frankfurt's 10–3 victory at San Antonio. Barcelona silenced 53,238 fans in Montreal as Gene Taylor's two touchdowns set up a 34–10 triumph for his side.

W E E K **2** S T A R S

PASSING
★ Kerwin Bell (Orlando) 29 of 44 for 341 yards, 4TDs
★ Jeff Graham (NY/NJ) 20 of 35 for 330 yards
★ Stan Gelbaugh (London) 24 of 40 for 326 yards, 1TD

RECEIVING
★ Monty Gilbreath (NY/NJ) 6 for 128 yards
★ Lonnie Turner (NY/NJ) 8 for 122 yards
★ Dana Brinson (London) 8 for 114 yards
★ Byron Williams (Orlando) 10 for 109 yards, 2TDs
★ John Simpson (Orlando) 7 for 103 yards, 2TDs

RUSHING
★ Eric Wilkerson (NY/NJ) 11 for 121 yards, 1TD

> ## WEEK THREE
> **RESULTS** (*Away team first*): Orlando
> Thunder **12**, London Monarchs **35**;
> Barcelona Dragons **26**, Raleigh-Durham
> Skyhawks **14**; Frankfurt Galaxy **27**, New
> York-New Jersey Knights **17**; Sacramento
> Surge **3**, San Antonio Riders **10**;
> Birmingham Fire **10**, Montreal Machine
> **23**.

ORLANDO THUNDER, the only unbeaten American side in the World League after two weeks of the season, arrived at Wembley with a reputation for a style of play as flashy as their fluorescent green shirts. By the time they left they had been made to look as ragged as a beaten army. The evening ended with a fierce outburst of patriotism brought about by a stunning performance by the Monarchs' very own London boy, running back Victor Ebubedike.

In what was now becoming an easy script for Monarchs fans to follow, London faltered early on and were lucky to escape only a field goal behind after punter Greg Horne had two efforts blocked deep inside London territory. But when the Monarchs finally clicked, they did so with spectacular results. A six-play touchdown drive ended with David Smith following Paul Berardelli's block into the end zone to give the Monarchs a lead which was never in jeopardy. With the tackling of Roy Hart anchoring the Monarchs' defensive line, the home side quickly embarked on a 64-yard scoring drive. Quarterback Stan Gelbaugh and receiver Tony Sargent produced the eye-catching stuff, connecting on a 38-yard touchdown. Another set of heroes also emerged in the form of the London offensive line – the Nasty Boyz – who allowed Gelbaugh to operate unmolested

Dana Brinson (81) receives protection from Victor Ebubedike (29) during a London kick return.

throughout virtually the entire game. Said coach Larry Kennan, 'With Orlando's explosive offense, it was vital that we keep them off the field and the Nasty Boyz made that happen. Stan received great protection from the offensive line all night.'

Charlie Baumann's 30-yard field goal for Orlando was scant consolation for a ball dropped in the end zone by Byron Williams. The Thunder were made to pay by Smith's fourth touchdown in three games and Jeff Alexander's first points for the Monarchs, leaving the home team enjoying a 28–6 advantage. Thunder quarterback Kerwin Bell's frustrations were eased slightly by a 39-yard touchdown pass to Chris Roscoe, but that merely set the stage for Ebubedike. Entering the game with the Monarchs facing third and seven from the Orlando 44, the Londoner charged through a huge hole on the right of the line for 11 yards. On the next play, he bounced off a tackle for 10 more. A three-yard run followed and then, evading two defenders, he went hell for leather for the corner of the end zone, only to be shoved out two yards shy. With the seconds ticking away, Ebubedike was stopped short again, but on the final offensive play of the game he dived over the goal line behind the blocking of Jeff Alexander and the crowd erupted as though the England soccer team had again won the World Cup.

'We sent Victor in to run out the clock,' explained Kennan, 'but then we said, "Let's go for it." The people who were most excited were the other guys on the team.' While Ebubedike inevitably attracted most of the attention, Kennan didn't forget the magnificent effort by the rest of the team. 'I've never been more proud of a bunch of players than today. That was as fine a football game as I've ever been involved with. We played great offense and defense.'

Orlando's Kerwin Bell was unable to make much noise against London.

Barcelona joined the Monarchs on the 3–0 mark as Thomas Woods' 27-yard scoring run clinched a 26–14 victory over winless Raleigh-Durham. Frankfurt underlined the early dominance of the European Division by winning 27–17 at New York-New Jersey, where the Knights fumbled 12 times and gained only 123 yards. Mike Johnson's eight-yard pass to Bill Hess was sufficient for San Antonio to beat Sacramento 10–3. Montreal's Richard Shelton scored on a 25-yard fumble return and a 63-yard interception return in a 23–10 defeat of Birmingham, earning Player of the Week honours.

WEEK 3 STARS

PASSING	★ Stan Gelbaugh (London) 24 of 41 for 315 yards, 1TD
	★ Mike Perez (Frankfurt) 22 of 36 for 261 yards, 3TDs
RECEIVING	★ Jason Johnson (Frankfurt) 5 for 103 yards, 1TD
RUSHING	★ Paul Palmer (Barcelona) 28 for 133 yards, 1TD

THE LONDON MONARCHS stepped impressively over a potential banana skin on their path to the World Bowl. The players ignored the distractions of returning to their native America for the first time in the season and produced a thoroughly professional and emphatic 27–0 beating of the Birmingham Fire.

It took only one drive for the Monarchs to demonstrate that neither jet lag nor emotional reunions with their families and loved ones could divert them from their single-minded intention to return to England, their adopted home, with an unbeaten record. Using their staple diet of short passes to running back Judd Garrett to eat up the yardage, the Monarchs advanced to David Smith's six-yard touchdown run. The combination of Garrett, who ended the night with a league-record 12 receptions, and Jon Horton, who again showed his

big-play ability with catches of 71 and 50 yards, set the table for Gelbaugh and receiver Andre Riley to devour the Birmingham defense. Meanwhile, Fire quarterback Brent Pease was left only crumbs by the sack-hungry Danny Lockett and Roy Hart and ended with just a slimline 65 yards to his credit.

Phil Alexander's 27-yard field goal was followed by a Dana Brinson punt return, which went 85 scintillating yards to the end zone – only to be ruled out by a yellow penalty flag. Gelbaugh made the game safe in the fourth quarter by linking with Riley for a pair of touchdowns. The first appeared destined never to happen when the London quarterback was grabbed near the halfway line by Darrell Phillips. But Gelbaugh broke free, rolled to his left and hoisted a 33-yard pass over the confused defense to the awaiting Riley. The second was a more orthodox play, Gelbaugh hitting Riley on a slant pattern from

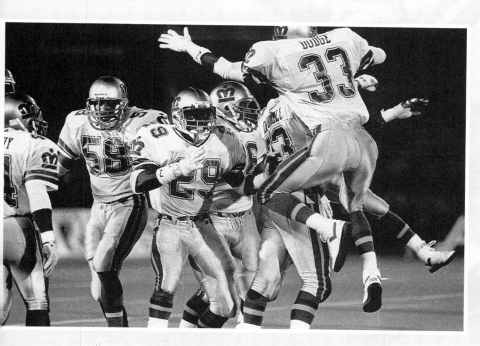

Dedrick Dodge (33) celebrates with teammates after the London Monarchs special teams force a turnover against the Birmingham Fire.

Overleaf: Dana Brinson (left) is upset by a disallowed touchdown, but a Firegirl (right) is happy.

13 yards. 'I don't know how I got away from the rush on the first one,' admitted Gelbaugh. 'I just saw Andre wide open and let it go. It was a duck, but it got there. On the second touchdown we read their defense and executed perfectly.'

Alexander completed the scoring with another 27-yard field goal, leaving coach Larry Kennan having to dismiss early talk of the World Bowl and play down his team's achievements. 'Everyone in the league is thinking we are supermen. But we have just been coaching the players hard and they have responded very, very well. They are a bunch of good athletes, they work hard so they play well.'

Lockett's two sacks took his tally to a league-leading eight in four games and highlighted a dominating display by the Monarchs defense. 'Our defense played a good game from start to finish,' said Kennan. 'We didn't even give them a breath of fresh air all night.'

New York-New Jersey ended their three-game losing streak with an overwhelming 44–0 thrashing of Montreal as Player of the Week Jeff Graham passed for three touchdowns. Barcelona continued their fast start when Scott Erney hit Gene Taylor for touchdowns of 56 and 81 yards on the way to a 33–13 victory over Orlando. A 66-yard fumble return from Kubi Kalombo set up Sacramento's 16–10 defeat of Frankfurt, while Raleigh-Durham wilted 37–15 in the face of 290 rushing yards by San Antonio.

WEEK 4 STARS

PASSING
★ Jeff Graham (NY/NJ) 18 of 30 for 411 yards, 3TDs
★ Scott Erney (Barcelona) 20 of 36 for 340 yards, 3TDs
★ Kerwin Bell (Orlando) 25 of 43 for 312 yards, 1TD
★ Stan Gelbaugh (London) 22 of 32 for 302 yards, 2TDs

RECEIVING
★ Kip Lewis (NY/NJ) 6 for 169 yards, 2TDs
★ Gene Taylor (Barcelona) 5 for 163 yards, 2TDs
★ Lonnie Turner (NY/NJ) 6 for 146 yards, 1TD

RUSHING
★ Ricky Blake (San Antonio) 21 for 140 yards, 1TD
★ Tony Baker (Frankfurt) 21 for 91 yards, 1TD

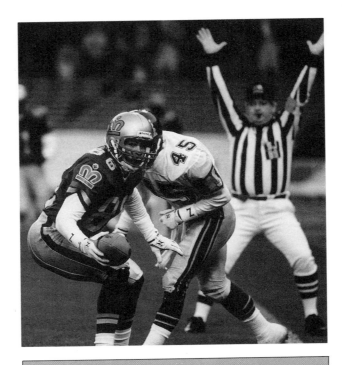

● **Jon Horton (86) beats Steve Lofton (45) for a London touchdown.**

WEEK FIVE

RESULTS (*Away team first*): Montreal Machine **7**, London Monarchs **45**; Raleigh-Durham Skyhawks **28**, Frankfurt Galaxy **30**; Barcelona Dragons **14**, San Antonio Riders **22**; Birmingham Fire **31**, Orlando Thunder **6**; Sacramento Surge **20**, New York-New Jersey Knights **28**.

THE LONDON MONARCHS dominated from the opening kick-off to the final gun as they dismantled the Montreal Machine with a six-touchdown performance to take sole possession of first place in the World League's European Division. A cold evening at Wembley turned out to be a benefit night for two players. Quarterback Stan Gelbaugh threw for four touchdowns in the 45–7 rout, and wide receiver Jon Horton scored three times and was unlucky to lose out to his team-mate for the league's Player of the Week award.

The Montreal defense actually managed to restrict London to a 22-yard field goal on the home team's first drive, but that was to be their one moral victory of the game. The Monarchs' defensive unit, meanwhile, were almost impenetrable. Danny Lockett's two sacks helped to restrict Montreal quarterback Michael Proctor to 149 yards, and Virgil

Robertson's interception triggered his team's first touchdown. Gelbaugh took advantage of the turnover by hitting Dana Brinson from 34 yards and following up with a tight spiral to Horton for a four-yard score. By half-time Gelbaugh, as well as scrambling 48 yards himself, had aired the ball out for Horton to give his defender the slip and score a 41-yard touchdown for a 17–0 lead.

In the locker room, coach Larry Kennan told his team to approach the second half as though the score was 0–0. Brinson obviously took his words to heart. As the third quarter opened, Brinson burst out from behind his wall of blockers and sprinted down the right touchline for a touchdown on a dazzling 93-yard kick-off return. After Ricky Johnson put Montreal on the board with a 20-yard sweep play, it was the turn of Judd Garrett and the Nasty Boyz to do their thing. The Monarchs running back turned a short screen

20
●

pass into a 40-yard score, thanks to the offensive linemen blazing a trail through the Machine defense. Horton's third touchdown reception, this one from 12 yards, capped a 10-play, 80-yard drive. Following the retirement of Gelbaugh to the bench. John Witkowski stepped in to complete the scoring with a lofted 22-yard pass to Tony Sargent – rounding off a memorable match for the Bomb Squad, the Monarchs' corps of wide receivers. 'Tonight was my night,' said Horton. 'Any time it could be any other person's night. That is the type of team we are. Our offense is explosive and I am just happy to be part of it.'

Brinson added, 'It was a very satisfying performance. We played well as a unit. It was a short week for us after getting back from the States and we did a good job under the circumstances. Jet lag set in a little bit, but in order to be 5–0 we knew we couldn't let it affect our performance.'

Gelbaugh made sure the Monarchs coaches received their share of credit. 'The coaches picked the right guys and they have done a great job preparing us,' he said. 'The guys have put in their time and studied.'

Barcelona failed to keep pace with London when San Antonio quarterback Jason and receiver John, brothers of Monarchs running back Judd Garrett, combined on a 43-yard touchdown to give their team a 22–14 victory over the Dragons. Frankfurt receiver Cedric Gordon denied Raleigh-Durham their first win with a seven-yard touchdown catch with 17 seconds remaining to give the Galaxy a 30–28 success. Birmingham took advantage of six Orlando turnovers to win 31–6, while New York-New Jersey quarterback Jeff Graham scored twice in a 28–20 defeat of Sacramento.

WEEK 5 STARS

PASSING ★ Stan Gelbaugh (London) 17 of 29 for 286 yards, 4TDs

RECEIVING ★ Willie Bouyer (Birmingham) 4 for 141 yards, 2TDs
★ Marvin Hargrove (Raleigh-Durham) 9 for 113 yards, 2TDs
★ Carl Parker (Sacramento) 6 for 106 yards, 1TD
★ Byron Williams (Orlando) 8 for 101 yards
★ Dwight Pickens (San Antonio) 2 for 101 yards, 1TD
★ Jon Horton (London) 6 for 88 yards, 3TDs

RUSHING ★ Eric Wilkerson (NY/NJ) 21 for 133 yards, 1TD
★ Tony Baker (Frankfurt) 23 for 112 yards, 1TD
★ Victor Floyd (Sacramento) 13 for 102 yards

WEEK SIX

RESULTS (*Away team first*): Montreal Machine **7**, Frankfurt Galaxy **17**; Barcelona Dragons **29**, Sacramento Surge **20** (OT); Orlando Thunder **6**, New York-New Jersey Knights **42**; Raleigh-Durham Skyhawks **10**, London Monarchs **35**; San Antonio Riders **12**, Birmingham Fire **16**.

MORE THAN 33,000 London Monarchs fans turned up at Wembley like Romans arriving to see the Christians thrown to the lions. In the end they were given the comfortable victory over the hapless Raleigh-Durham Skyhawks they had predicted. But it took a crucial defensive play early in the second half to quell a surprisingly spirited uprising from a team who plainly did not realise what was expected of them.

Far from timidly surrendering against the World League's only unbeaten side, the Skyhawks had the cheek to force a fumble from David Smith on the first play of the game and take the lead through Wilson Hoyle's 33-yard field goal. The Monarchs offense needed until their third drive to show their true colours when Judd Garrett and Tony Sargent caught important passes before Stan Gelbaugh's one-yard scoring toss to Jeff Alexander. The Skyhawks response was an emphatic one, an 80-yard touchdown drive which ended with John Burch finally beating some determined London tackling to force his way into the end zone from two yards. Four Monarchs plays later, however, the home side led 14–10. Gelbaugh reeled off a series of superb passes, the final one finding Andre Riley in the seam between the cornerback and safety for a 25-yard touchdown.

Raleigh-Durham stunned the Monarchs on the first play of the second half when quarterback Bobby McAllister found Melvin Patterson downfield for a gain of 72 yards, putting the Skyhawks within three yards of regaining the lead. Burch accounted for two, but when McAllister tried to make the final yard the ball was knocked from his grasp and finished up in the possession of Monarchs nose tackle Roy Hart. Instead of being 17–14 up, the Skyhawks quickly found that the game was beyond them. Alexander sliced through from 13 yards, Gelbaugh found Sargent from eight yards for his third touchdown pass, and Smith rounded off the entertainment with a three-yard run for the Monarchs' fifth touchdown.

● *Left:* **Monarchs receiver Dana Brinson fails to hold on to a Stan Gelbaugh pass.**

● *Right:* **Monarchs running back Judd Garrett attempts to break free for a big gain against the Raleigh-Durham Skyhawks.**

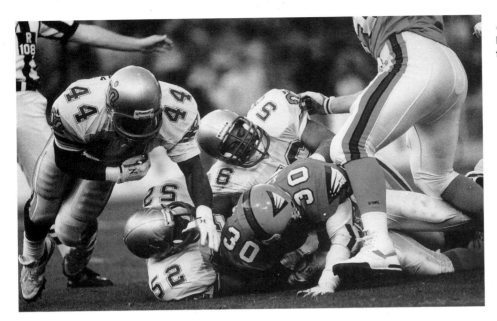

Skyhawks running back Bren Lowery is gang tackled by the Monarchs.

'That was a very big play,' said Kennan of the third-quarter turnover. 'It was a great defensive play and then we were able to go straight down and stick it in their end zone for a 14-point turnaround.' As well as that fumble recovery, the 293 lb figure of Hart was responsible for two sacks, a forced fumble and four unassisted tackles. 'Roy came up big for us,' Kennan continued. 'He is such a physical player that at the end of the night the guy across the line from him is going to know he has been through a war.'

The Monarchs' final touchdown proved to be costly. Smith, in straining to reach the end zone, damaged ligaments in his left knee and would not play again until the play-offs. Nevertheless, after win number six it was a confident Monarchs party which set off for what general manager Billy Hicks

described as 'the mother of all road trips' – three games across the Atlantic in the space of two weeks.

Barcelona clinched victory in the league's first overtime game when Eric Naposki returned an interception 27 yards for a touchdown to beat Sacramento 29–20. Meanwhile, European rivals Frankfurt took their record to 4–2 as Jason Johnson caught two Mike Perez touchdown passes in a 17–7 triumph against Montreal. Eric Wilkerson's hat-trick of touchdowns set up New York-New Jersey's 42–6 thrashing of Orlando, while a pair of Steve Avery scores were decisive in Birmingham's 16–12 win against San Antonio. Knights defensive end Tony Woods and Fire linebacker John Brantley were joint Players of the Week.

W E E K 6 S T A R S

PASSING ★ Stan Gelbaugh (London) 29 of 39 for 361 yards, 3TDs

RECEIVING ★ Demetrius Davis (Barcelona) 9 for 116 yards
★ Willie Snead (Montreal) 5 for 109 yards, 1TD
★ Cornell Burbage (NY/NJ) 3 for 107 yards
★ Carl Parker (Sacramento) 7 for 106 yards, 1TD
★ Jason Johnson (Frankfurt) 5 for 102 yards, 2TDs
★ Judd Garrett (London) 10 for 91 yards

RUSHING ★ Jim Bell (Barcelona) 31 for 130 yards
★ Eric Wilkerson (NY/NJ) 14 for 56 yards, 3TDs

WEEK SEVEN RESULTS (*Away team first*): Birmingham Fire **6**, Barcelona Dragons **11**; Montreal Machine **26**, Sacramento Surge **23** (OT); Frankfurt Galaxy **17**, Orlando Thunder **14**; New York-New Jersey Knights **42**, Raleigh-Durham Skyhawks **6**; London Monarchs **38**, San Antonio Riders **15**.

JUST WHEN it seemed that the London Monarchs' unbeaten record might be in jeopardy, Larry Kennan's team lit up San Antonio's Alamo Stadium with an outburst of offense that produced 38 points in little over 17 minutes. It ensured that the Monarchs finished the first leg of their American adventure with a perfect 7–0 record.

Trailing 9–0 after the first quarter, the Monarchs faced the prospect of their first truly competitive game since the second week of the season. Then Jeff Alexander rushed for two touchdowns and Stan Gelbaugh threw for three more to produce yet another one-sided scoreline of 38–15. After seeing his side score on six successive possessions, coach Kennan confessed, 'We were scoring so fast there, it made my head start to swivel looking at the scoreboard.'

'Our team showed their true colours tonight', he continued. 'We didn't panic after falling behind. We knew San Antonio would be a tough team, but we made some adjustments and some big plays.'

The Riders, who were responsible for inflicting Barcelona's only defeat during the first six weeks of the season, built an early lead. Ricky Blake dashed in from 13 yards and Anthony Cooney added a safety by tackling new Monarchs running back J. J. Flannigan,

Monarchs linebacker Marlon Brown (53) gets to grips with San Antonio's dangerous running back Ricky Blake (23).

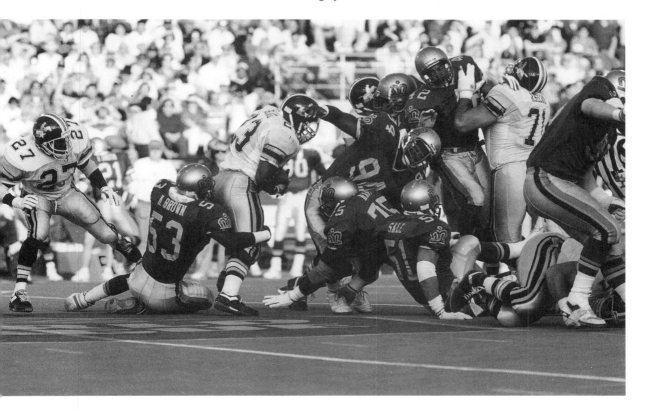

picked up from Orlando as a replacement for the injured David Smith. Then London hit back. Gelbaugh completed seven out of eight passes on an 80-yard drive before handing off to Alexander for a scoring run of eight yards. A Riders fumble paved the way for Jon Horton to catch Gelbaugh's seven-yard pass just inside the end zone. There was still time before the end of the first half for Dedrick Dodge to return an overthrown pass from Riders quarterback Jason Garrett 62 yards to the San Antonio five-yard line. From there Alexander sprinted in for his fourth touchdown in two games.

The Monarchs' blitz continued in the third quarter as Andre Riley's 22-yard gain on a reverse allowed Gelbaugh to drill a six-yard pass into the arms of Horton for a 28–9 lead. It took one play for London to regain possession. Marlon Brown's fumble recovery put Gelbaugh in a position to throw his 11th consecutive complete pass, a nine-yard touchdown strike on the run to Tony Sargent. Yet another Riders turnover followed, although this time the Monarchs had to make do with Phil Alexander kicking a 38-yard field goal. The only further scoring was a consolation touchdown reception from San Antonio's Dwight Pickens. Riders linebacker Mark Ledbetter tried to explain the Monarchs' dominance. 'They came out with good field position all night and managed to execute offensively,' he said. 'We knew what they were going to do, but they still did it.'

Despite being outgained 272 yards to 253, the Monarchs forced four decisive turnovers, leaving Kennan to conclude, 'All season our defense have come up with big plays when we needed them. It seems like most times when we take over possession our offense starts with excellent field position.'

Having lost their opening three games, New York-New Jersey reeled off their fourth straight win with a crushing 42–6 defeat of Raleigh-Durham, who were limited to only 122 total yards. Meanwhile, Birmingham failed to take a clear lead in the North American West Division when they turned the ball over on six of their final eight possessions in losing 11–6 at Barcelona. Frankfurt scored 14 points in the final quarter to complete a 17–14 victory over Orlando, while Montreal's Richard Shelton returned a punt and a kick-off for touchdowns and Bjorn Nittmo landed an overtime field goal for a 26–23 triumph against Sacramento. Frankfurt's Tony Baker was named Player of the Week.

Riders receiver Elliott Searcy is brought down by Monarchs linebacker Virgil Robertson (55).

W E E K	7	S T A R S	
PASSING	★ Mike Perez (Frankfurt) 20 of 33 for 346 yards, 1TD		
	★ Mike Elkins (Sacramento) 16 of 39 for 300 yards, 2TDs		
	★ Tony Rice (Barcelona) 20 of 25 for 254 yards		
RECEIVING	★ Tony Baker (Frankfurt) 7 for 173 yards		
RUSHING	★ Eric Wilkerson (NY/NJ) 16 for 91 yards		

San Antonio Riders quarterback Jason Garrett (left) is sacked by London Monarchs linebacker Marlon Brown during the Monarchs' 38—15 victory.

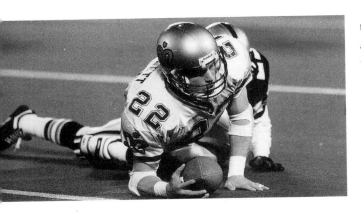

IF ANY SINGLE game during the course of the season proved that the London Monarchs possessed the stuff of which champions are made, it was their 22–7 victory at Giants Stadium. They knew that the New York-New Jersey Knights would be brimming with confidence after four successive wins and eager for revenge after their Wembley defeat. They knew, from comments in the New York newspapers, that the Knights players really didn't like them very much and would be out to intimidate them. What they hadn't expected was the hostility of the 41,219 crowd, who spent the entire evening pelting the Monarchs players with cans, drink cartons, food, ice cubes and spittle. They even launched an assault – thankfully only a verbal one – at the cheerleaders, The Crown Jewels, who had been flown in from London for the match.

In that kind of environment the game, predictably, turned out to be probably the most intense, emotional and bad-tempered contest of the season. In such a war of attrition – and with quarterback Stan Gelbaugh missing the second half with an injured shoulder – it was always going to be up to the Monarchs defense to fire the winning shots. And how magnificently they rallied to their task. By the end of the game, Knights quarterback Jeff Graham must have felt like he had been trampled over by an entire infantry unit. Sacked a professional football record 14 times, he struck up an intimate relationship with the artificial turf as he ended almost every play sprawled on his back.

Yet despite the efforts of running back Jeff Alexander, who rushed determinedly for 128 yards and scored a 41-yard touchdown to give the Monarchs a 9–0 lead following Phil Alexander's first half field goal, the London defense were called upon for one last heroic stand inside the final two minutes. Having seen their lead cut to 9–7 by Eric Wilkerson's three-yard score, the Monarchs handed their opponents an opportunity to win the game when they were forced to punt with 1:47 remaining. But on the second play of

Above: Running back Judd Garrett struggles to gain the extra yards during the London Monarchs' victory against the Knights.

Right: Monarchs defensive end John Shannon is a casualty of his team's brutal battle in New York.

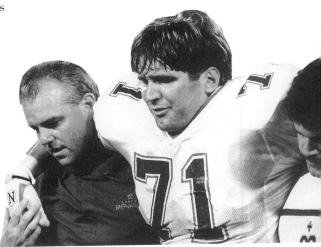

The London Monarchs' cheerleaders, The Crown Jewels, meet their counterparts from the New York-New Jersey Knights.

e decisive drive Graham overthrew a pass straight into the arms of Monarchs safety Dedrick Dodge, who ced unopposed down the right sideline and dived iumphantly into the end zone for a touchdown. here was just time for the Monarchs defense, later amed joint Players of the Week by the league, to rub lt into the Knights' gaping wound. Linebacker arlon 'Space Dog' Brown blitzed Graham yet again, king his personal tally of sacks to five and a half d giving team-mate Danny Lockett the chance to ck up the fumbled ball and set off for a 65-yard uchdown. 'It was a very physical, emotional game,' id coach Larry Kennan over the din of wild locker om celebrations. 'It got downright nasty out there at nes, but we kept our composure. This is a pivotal n for us, a huge win. Our defense was unbelievable.' Lockett claimed the Monarchs' defensive tactics – launch an all-out attack on Graham – had rprised their opponents. 'We showed them the blitz d I don't think they really expected it. We usually

just rush three defensive linemen or three linemen and one linebacker. This time we put in a full blitz.' Lockett concluded, 'After all the talk we proved we're the number one defense and we proved we're the better team.' No one was about to argue with Lockett and Co. – least of all Jeff Graham.

Barcelona stubbornly stayed on London's tail in the European Division by beating San Antonio 17–7, Gene Taylor scoring the decisive touchdown on a 35-yard reception from Tony Rice. Orlando running back Eric Mitchel scored three times as his team kept their play-off hopes alive with a 45–33 win against Sacramento, while Montreal went joint top of the North American East Division when K. D. Dunn's touchdown sealed a 15–6 victory over Raleigh-Durham. Frankfurt quarterback Mike Perez directed a 98-yard touchdown drive to secure his team's 10–3 defeat of Birmingham.

WEEK 8 STARS

PASSING ★ Mike Elkins (Sacramento) 23 of 41 for 338 yards, 2TDs

RECEIVING ★ Gene Taylor (Barcelona) 5 for 129 yards, 1TD

RUSHING ★ Jeff Alexander (London) 21 for 128 yards, 1TD
★ Eric Mitchel (Orlando) 12 for 108 yards, 3TDs

WEEK NINE

RESULTS (*Away team first*): London Monarchs **45**, Sacramento Surge **21**; Frankfurt Galaxy **10**, Barcelona Dragons **3**; Montreal Machine **10**, San Antonio Riders **27**; New York-New Jersey Knights **14**, Birmingham Fire **24**; Orlando Thunder **20**, Raleigh-Durham Skyhawks **14**.

● London Monarchs safety Dedrick Dodge had good reason to celebrate in Sacramento, his 60-yard interception return for a touchdown completing a spectacular three-game road trip.

AFTER OWING a debt of gratitude to their defense in New York, the London Monarchs produced an offensive explosion to clinch their place in the World League semi-finals. Their 45–21 victory over Sacramento was in the bag as early as the second quarter. Wide receiver Jon Horton produced a record-breaking performance, gaining 196 yards on eight catches and overtaking the previous best of 173 yards before half-time. Hardly surprising that the league made him their Player of the Week.

Stan Gelbaugh, on his way to gaining 325 yards, threw a perfect pass just out of the reach of a defender for Horton to open the scoring with a 30-yard touchdown. After Ken Sale's one-handed interception, Jeff Alexander scored the first of his three touchdowns by breaking clear from 40 yards out. Horton proved he possessed the strength to go with his safe hands when he set up the next touchdown. Catching Gelbaugh's pass, Horton bounced off two tackles before his 22-yard gain was brought to a halt at the one-yard line. From there Alexander happily took over to round off a drive which had begun back at the London 16. Phil Alexander's 25-yard field goal made it 24–0, before the irrespressible Dedrick Dodge, enjoying a spectacular road trip, stepped inside Surge running back Victor Floyd to intercept Mike Elkins' pass and gallop unopposed to a 60-yard touchdown.

Sacramento finally put some points on the board with the final play of the first half as Carl Sumner held on to Elkins' 41-yard desperation pass. The Monarchs marched 76 yards on the first drive of the second half, Jeff Alexander scoring his eighth touchdown in four games by sweeping around right end from three yards. The London onslaught at last began to ease up and John Witkowski's 10-yard pass to a diving Dana Brinson – sandwiched between

touchdown receptions from Sacramento's Mel Farr and Carl Parker – was their only other score.

Having become the Monarchs' latest victims, it was the turn of the Surge staff to attempt to explain London's dominance over the rest of the league. Coach Kay Stephenson ventured, 'We were soundly beaten because they are well coached and well disciplined. They were the best team we've played all-round – offensively, defensively and on special teams. You'd like to rush the ball 25 or 30 times a game, but they took that option away from us.'

Horton, meanwhile, accounted for his outstanding performance by praising quarterback Gelbaugh. 'Stan did his usual excellent job of putting the ball right where I like it,' he said. 'He is excellent at hitting you when you have the chance to do something big. Our chemistry is outstanding.' Now only the Barcelona Dragons at Wembley stood between the Monarchs and a perfect 10–0 regular season record. 'Teams are starting to gun for us,' said Horton, 'but with the character of our team it won't happen.'

● The Monarchs arrived back in London to discover they were European Division champions, thanks to Barcelona being beaten 10–3 at home by Frankfurt, who now needed just to win their final game to gain a wild-card place in the semi-finals. One touchdown – a six-yard catch by Tony Baker – was sufficient for the Galaxy. San Antonio came from behind to beat Montreal 27–10 and stay in the play-off picture as Ricky Blake scored two touchdowns, but Birmingham maintained pole position in the North American West Division by beating New York-New Jersey 24–14. The Knights' defeat kept the door open for Orlando, who were put on their way to a 20–14 defeat of Raleigh-Durham by Erroll Tucker's 95-yard touchdown on the opening kick-off return.

W E E K   **9**   S T A R S

PASSING   ★ Stan Gelbaugh (London) 18 of 26 for 325 yards, 1TD

RECEIVING   ★ Jon Horton (London) 8 for 196 yards, 1TD
              ★ Carl Parker (Sacramento) 11 for 136 yards, 1TD
              ★ Clarkston Hines (Raleigh-Durham) 6 for 117 yards, 1TD
              ★ Lee Morris (San Antonio) 5 for 109 yards, 1TD

RUSHING   ★ Tony Baker (Frankfurt) 23 for 96 yards
              ★ Jeff Alexander (London) 4 for 44 yards, 3TDs

WEEK TEN

RESULTS (*Away team first*):
Sacramento Surge **24**, Frankfurt Galaxy **13**; Birmingham Fire **28**, Raleigh-Durham Skyhawks **7**; San Antonio Riders **9**, New York-New Jersey Knights **38**; Barcelona Dragons **20**, London Monarchs **17**; Orlando Thunder **33**, Montreal Machine **27** (OT).

FOR ONCE, the Dragons' fire could not be extinguished by the English. The London Monarchs' hopes of becoming the first pro football team to go through a season unbeaten since the NFL's Miami Dolphins in 1972 died in front of a 50,835 crowd at Wembley Stadium.

In the end, victory went to the team which desired it more. While the Monarchs were secure in the knowledge they were already in the semi-finals, the Barcelona Dragons took the field at the famous old stadium having been given an unexpected reprieve by Frankfurt Galaxy's shock defeat at home to Sacramento. A win would give them an 8–2 record, the best among the three division runners-up, and a berth in the play-offs. A fraction of a second quicker at the snap of the ball, marginally more determined in their blocking and tackling and more able than the Monarchs to come up with big plays at vital moments, the Dragons led 17–3 after three quarters – a big enough cushion to withstand the home team's late rally. 'We weren't as ready to play as they were,' admitted London coach Larry Kennan. 'We had a chance at several stages to turn the game, but we didn't get it done. They executed better than we did and we didn't do most things as well as we have been. No question, there was more at stake for them than us, but it's still not a good reason to lose.'

The Monarchs were given every incentive for victory by the spine-tingling reception they were given by their fans on their first Wembley appearance for a month. Those cheers had barely receded before London punter Greg Horne was having his kick

● **Dragons receiver Thomas Woods (left) comes under pressure from** **London safety Dan Crossman.**

● **Monarchs linebacker Danny Lockett (94) brings Dragons running back Jim** **Bell down to earth with a fierce tackle.**

blocked deep in Monarchs territory and the Dragons were cashing in with Massimo Manca's 22-yard field goal. With quarterback Stan Gelbaugh experiencing the kind of pressure he had hitherto been successfully shielded from all season, the Monarchs failed to make inroads into the Dragons defense. After Horne's disastrous punt went only nine yards, Barcelona quarterback Scott Erney found tight end Demetrius Davis leaping above cornerback Corris Ervin for a 28-yard touchdown. Phil Alexander's 39-yard field goal, making the score 10–3, produced the only points of the second quarter. The Dragons proceeded to extend their advantage to 14 points when sloppy tackling from Ervin and Dedrick Dodge allowed Davis to turn a short pass from Erney into a 36-yard score.

Andre Riley finally ignited the Monarchs offense with a superb 40-yard gain, leaving Jeff Alexander only one yard to cover for his 10th touchdown of the season. But it was Alexander who fumbled minutes later to set up a Dragons drive that took up seven and a half precious minutes and ended with Manca kicking a 20-yard field goal. Riley again raised the Monarchs' hopes by combining with Gelbaugh for 53 yards, and on the next play Jon Horton was on the

end of a 12-yard touchdown pass to leave Barcelona three points up with less than three minutes remaining. But the Dragons offense broke the hearts of the London fans by twice converting crucial third-down plays to retain possession and deny the Monarchs the chance to wipe out their lead. 'They came in with a great gameplan, to control the clock, and they did it,' admitted Dodge. 'When they needed five yards they got it and when they had to go deep they did it. We wanted to be 10–0, but we'll be back.'

Frankfurt blew their semi-final hopes when they became the only European team to be beaten at home by an American side all season, Carl Parker's two touchdown receptions helping Sacramento to a 24–13 victory that stunned the Waldstadion's 51,653 crowd. Birmingham clinched the North American West Division by gaining 168 rushing yards in a 28–7 win against Raleigh-Durham, who ended the season winless. New York-New Jersey became North American West champions after three second-quarter touchdowns softened up San Antonio for a 38–9 beating, making Orlando's 33–27 overtime victory in Montreal meaningless. Barcelona's Demetrius Davis won the Player of the Week award.

Jeff Alexander (20)
battles for a touchdown.

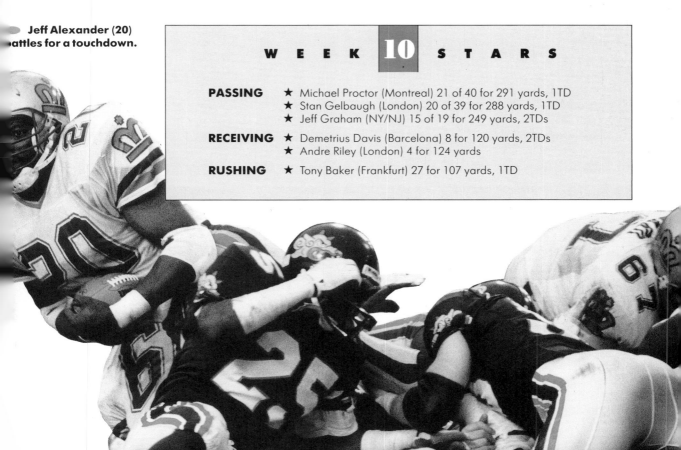

W E E K	**10**	S T A R S
PASSING	★ Michael Proctor (Montreal) 21 of 40 for 291 yards, 1TD	
	★ Stan Gelbaugh (London) 20 of 39 for 288 yards, 1TD	
	★ Jeff Graham (NY/NJ) 15 of 19 for 249 yards, 2TDs	
RECEIVING	★ Demetrius Davis (Barcelona) 8 for 120 yards, 2TDs	
	★ Andre Riley (London) 4 for 124 yards	
RUSHING	★ Tony Baker (Frankfurt) 27 for 107 yards, 1TD	

FINAL REGULAR SEASON STANDINGS 1991

EUROPEAN DIVISION

	W	L	T	Pct	PF	PA
London Monarchs	9	1	0	.900	310	121
Barcelona Dragons	8	2	0	.800	206	126
Frankfurt Galaxy	7	3	0	.700	155	139

NORTH AMERICAN DIVISION

	W	L	T	Pct	PF	PA
NY/NJ Knights	5	5	0	.500	257	155
Orlando Thunder	5	5	0	.500	242	286
Montreal Machine	4	6	0	.400	145	244
Raleigh-Durham Skyhawks	0	10	0	.000	123	300

NORTH AMERICAN WEST DIVISION

	W	L	T	Pct	PF	PA
Birmingham Fire	5	5	0	.500	140	140
San Antonio Riders	4	6	0	.400	176	196
Sacramento Surge	3	7	0	.300	179	226

REGULAR SEASON ATTENDANCE

TEAM	TOTAL	AVERAGE	LARGEST
London	202,405	40,481	50,835
New York-New Jersey	161,898	32,380	41,219
Montreal	159,441	31,882	53,238
Frankfurt	149,281	29,856	51,653
Barcelona	145,011	29,002	40,875
Birmingham	127,500	25,500	53,000
Orlando	97,687	19,537	24,309
Sacramento	89,971	17,994	21,409
San Antonio	74,266	14,853	20,234
Raleigh-Durham	60,329	12,066	17,900
WORLD LEAGUE	1,267,789	24,280	53,238

1991 ALL-WORLD LEAGUE TEAM
(SELECTED BY THE HEAD COACHES)

FIRST TEAM OFFENSE		**SECOND TEAM OFFENSE**
Jon Horton, London Gene Taylor, Barcelona Byron Williams, Orlando	WR- TE	Carl Parker, Sacramento Dana Brinson, London Monty Gilbreath, NY/NJ
Mike Withycombe, Orlando Steve Gabbard, London	T	Theo Adams, London Scott Adams, Barcelona
Garry Frank, Frankfurt Paul Berardelli, London	G	Barry Voorhees, Barcelona John Guerrero, Orlando
Doug Marrone, London	C	Curtis Wilson, Sacramento
Stan Gelbaugh, London	QB	Scott Erney, Barcelona
Ricky Blake, San Antonio Tony Baker, Frankfurt	RB	Eric Wilkerson, NY/NJ Judd Garrett, London Eric Mitchel, Orlando

FIRST TEAM DEFENSE		**SECOND TEAM DEFENSE**
Bruce Clark, Barcelona Mark Mraz, Frankfurt	DE	Donnie Gardner, San Antonio Shawn Knight, Sacramento
Roy Hart, London	NT	Mike Teeter, Frankfurt Darrell Phillips, Birmingham
Danny Lockett, London Tracy Simien, Montreal	OLB	Ron Sancho, NY/NJ Marlon Brown, London
John Brantley, Birmingham Tim Walton, San Antonio	ILB	Ken Sale, London Pete Najarian, Sacramento Ron Goetz, Barcelona
Anthony Parker, NY/NJ Corris Ervin, London	CB	Richard Shelton, Montreal John Holland, Birmingham
Greg Couauette, Sacramento	SS	Tim Broady, Frankfurt
John Miller, Birmingham	FS	Dedrick Dodge, London

FIRST TEAM SPECIALISTS		**SECOND TEAM SPECIALISTS**
Chris Mohr, Montreal	P	Kirk Maggio, Birmingham
Phil Alexander, London	K	Bjorn Nittmo, Montreal
Erroll Tucker, Orlando	ST	Richard Shelton, Montreal
Phil Alexander, London	Op.Dis.	Victor Ebubedike, London

London Monarchs wide receiver Jon Horton celebrates the 78-yard touchdown which clinched his team's semi-final victory against the New York-New Jersey Knights.

SEMI-FINALS
RESULTS (*Away team first*):
Barcelona Dragons **10**, Birmingham Fire
3 (Attendance: 40,500); London Monarchs
42, New York-New Jersey Knights **26**
(Attendance: 23,149).

SO THE FIRST ever World Bowl would have to
go ahead at Wembley Stadium without the home
team, the London Monarchs. At least, that's how it
looked five minutes into the second quarter of a
dramatic semi-final play-off at New Jersey's Giants
Stadium. It had been a big enough blow for the
Monarchs to have to concede their hard-earned home

Left: Battered Knights
uarterback Jeff Graham
uffers at the hands of
ondon's Danny Lockett.

Below: Party time for
the Monarchs as they
celebrate their
remarkable semi-final
victory at Giants Stadium.

Above: **Phil Alexander misses another field goal.**

advantage in the semi-finals because of Wembley's unavailability. It had been even worse when, having been ordered by the league to play away rather than at an alternative English venue, the Monarchs found themselves having to return to the cauldron of the New York-New Jersey Knights' home stadium. And now, worst of all, the Monarchs looked like missing out on the chance to become the World League's first champions as the Meadowlands scoreboard boasted a 17–0 Knights lead.

In their biggest game of the season, the Monarchs almost flawless all season long, finally looked as though they were coming unravelled. A Stan Gelbaugh interception gave the Knights the chance to go ahead through a 33-yard Kendall Trainor field goal. A Gelbaugh fumble after being sacked triggered a Knights drive which ended with Jeff Graham's 13-yard touchdown toss to Kip Lewis. Then Dedrick Dodge's failure to shove Lewis out of bounds allowed the New York receiver to complete a 49-yard reception for another touchdown.

Right: **Knights quarterback Jeff Graham feels the force of Monarchs defensive end Mike Renna.**

Above: **Monarchs hero Jon Horton makes a vital catch as the New York-New Jersey Knights close in.**

On the London bench, the shell-shocked Monarc
players wore expressions of utter disbelief. They ha
been through too much together, however, to let the
dreams die in such an inglorious fashion. As wide
receiver Jon Horton would explain later, 'We said to
each other, "Let's get our act together. We don't wan
to go out like suckers." You put us in a corner and w
are going to come out and fight like cats.' The

Jeff Graham gets his pass away despite the presence of the London Monarchs defense.

American television explores every angle in its search for a story. Monarchs offensive lineman Paul Berardelli is caught lying down on the job before the semi-final battle in New York.

Monarchs offense marched back onto the field and within six plays the feet of Jeff Alexander and the hands of Andre Riley had taken them to the Knights' six-yard line, from where Gelbaugh found Riley again, this time inches inside the end zone. A pair of catches from Horton put Gelbaugh in position to lob a 21-yard touchdown pass to Judd Garrett. Despite Trainor kicking a 48-yard field goal to make it 20–14

at half-time, the Monarchs appeared to have passed crisis point.

The Monarchs went ahead early in the third quarter when Horton made an astonishing finger-tip catch to set up Gelbaugh's one-yard play-action pass to tight end Pat Davis. It was quickly 28–20 as Horton climbed above two defenders to claim Gelbaugh's pass and then high-stepped into the end

zone for a 68-yard score. Eric Wilkerson's six-yard run, followed by a failed two-point conversion, pulled the Knights back to 28–26, but quarterback Graham was taking his usual beating at the hands of the Monarchs defense, who sacked him nine more times – five of them shared between Danny Lockett and Roy Hart. However, three missed field goals by Phil Alexander prevented the Monarchs putting the game away and it took an interception from the alert Corris Ervin deep in London territory to preserve their lead with less than four minutes to play. But then came the coaching call of the season when, faced with third and one at their own 22, the Monarchs were expected to make sure of continued possession by running the ball. Instead, Larry Kennan called for Gelbaugh to

dump the ball over the middle of the field to Horton, who sprinted away from a stunned Knights defense for a 78-yard touchdown. David Smith, fit again after his knee injury, scored from three yards in the dying seconds for a final score of 42–26.

Monarchs general manager Billy Hicks admitted, 'My stomach was doing flip-flops all through the game. But these guys had faith in themselves so all I could do was sit back and have faith as well.'

Barcelona booked their place at Wembley when Thomas Woods scored on a six-yard pass from Scott Erney and the Dragons defense forced six turnovers to preserve their 10–3 lead in Birmingham.

Left: Monarchs' Jon Horton races away from the New York-New Jersey defense to score his crucial 78-yard touchdown.

Above: Marlon Brown (53) and Mike Renna (right) halt the progress of the Knights.

SEMI-FINAL STATISTICS

LONDON PASSING   ★ Gelbaugh 25-42-391-5TDs

NY/NJ PASSING   ★ Graham 19-35-399-2TDs

LONDON RECEIVING   ★ Horton 8-225-2TDs; Riley 6-78-1TD; Garrett 5-56-1TD; Brinson 3–7; Sargent 2-24; Davis 1-1-1TD

NY/NJ RECEIVING   ★ Lewis 9-245-2TDs; Burbage 3-51; Turner 3-32; Gilbreath 2-44; Wilkerson 1-18; Jeffery 1–9

LONDON RUSHING   ★ J. Alexander 21-123; D. Smith 4-16-1TD; Gelbaugh 1-10

NY/NJ RUSHING   ★ Wilkerson 10-47-1TD; Graham 4–24; Jeffery 1-3

WORLD BOWL
SUNDAY JUNE 9, 1991,
WEMBLEY STADIUM
Barcelona Dragons **0**
London Monarchs **21**
(Attendance 61,108).

THE LONDON MONARCHS were crowned champions of the World League amid emotional scenes of celebration that demonstrated just how quickly and how completely Britain's newest sporting stars had won a place in the hearts of their public. As the players paraded the World Bowl trophy around Wembley Stadium to a background of 'Land of Hope and Glory', most of Queen's greatest hits and the team's own rap record, 'Yo Go Monarchs', it mattered little to the fans that their team's 21–0 victory had been in the bank at half-time – or that it had been earned by a display of rock-solid defense rather than

⬭ **Below:** Trevor Carthy (44), one of the London Monarchs' four British players, and David Caldwell (73) combine on a tackle during the World Bowl.

⬭ **Inset:** Monarchs offensive lineman Larry Jones explodes onto the Wembley field at the start of another evening of colourful entertainment at Britain's most famous sporting venue.

⬭ **Bottom right:** Monarchs wide receiver Jon Horton (right) beats Barcelona Dragons defensive back Charles Fryar to the ball on his way to a spectacular 59-yard touchdown to open the scoring in the World Bowl.

dazzling offense. All that concerned them was that this group of mostly Americans, who had been unknown to them three months earlier and would be back across the Atlantic in a day or two, had made London the champion city of the world.

General manager Billy Hicks, the man whose task it had been to put the Monarchs organisation together from scratch, admitted he had never dared imagine such a night and such a response. 'I have never had a better feeling inside than I had running around that field with our football team, feeling the adoration from the fans that was pouring out on to the field. It was unbelievable.'

That same adjective was used by London safety Dan Crossman, one of the more unsung Monarchs heroes during the season. He rose to the challenge of

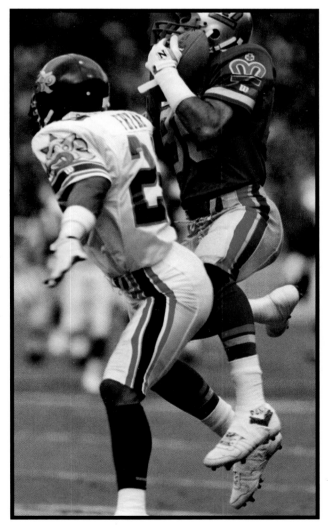

the biggest game of his career with three interceptions, including one for a touchdown, and four bone-jarring tackles to earn a new car after being voted Most Valuable Player. 'You never dare dream about doing something like this,' he confessed, 'especially in a game of this magnitude. Ever since training camp we have been talking about winning the world championship and I just wanted to help make it a reality.'

The Monarchs defense were in charge from the moment the Dragons messed up a field goal attempt on their first drive of the game – and with the Monarchs offense able to gain only 245 yards all night, the defense needed to be in control. Both

●Stan Gelbaugh with the
World Bowl trophy.

Monarchs drives had ended in punts when quarterback Stan Gelbaugh lined his team up at the London 41 with time about to expire in the first quarter. Throughout the season, when Gelbaugh needed a big play he looked for Jon Horton, and this time his favourite receiver obliged by leaving a defender floundering on the grass on his way to a stunning 59-yard touchdown. This was Crossman's cue to step forward into the spotlight. He picked off Scott Erney's first pass of the second quarter. On the Dragons' next possession, he stepped up in front of the intended Dragons receiver as Erney attempted a short pass to the left. Crossman lifted the ball triumphantly aloft as he strode into the end zone for a 20-yard touchdown. Crossman was in position for yet another interception to begin a drive which produced a touchdown for Judd Garrett on a delicate three-yard pass from Gelbaugh. By half-time, with the Monarchs 21–0 up and Erney having been intercepted four times – compared with twice during the entire regular season – the victory party had already started in the stands. By the end of a defense-dominated second half, during which back-up Barcelona quarterback Tony Rice was halted by Dedrick Dodge as he tried to scramble into the end zone, the celebrations were in full swing all around the stadium.

'The fact that we are going to wear rings that say "World Champions" is a great tribute to the players, coaches and the whole Monarchs organisation,' said coach Larry Kennan. 'This is my biggest thrill in coaching. I can't say enough about our assistant coaches and the job they have done, but without great players you can't win big games and we certainly have great players.' On this day Crossman definitely fitted into that category, and Kennan observed, 'He's been an outstanding player all season. He's a smart, intelligent, tough player and if anybody deserves to win an MVP award it is Dan Crossman – there isn't a better team guy than him. All our guys deserve all the credit and accolades that are coming to them.' The first World League season may not have ended with the classic down-to-the-wire game most people had hoped for, but no one at Wembley Stadium seemed to mind. Indeed, Kennan spoke for all 61,108 fans by saying, 'If that wasn't big-time football out there, then I've never seen it.'

🔵 **Above: Monarchs safety Dan Crossman receives the World Bowl MVP award after** intercepting three passes and scoring a touchdown against Barcelona.

WORLD BOWL STATISTICS

BARCELONA PASSING ★ Erney 7-17-102; Rice 10-24-165

LONDON PASSING ★ Gelbaugh 18-25-191-2TDs; Witkowski 1-2-6

BARCELONA RECEIVING ★ Davis 6-83; Taylor 4–93; Woods 3-44; Carr 1-19; Egerton 1-14; Norman 1-11; Bell 1-3

LONDON RECEIVING ★ Garrett 13-99-1TD; Riley 5-39; Horton 1-59-1TD

BARCELONA RUSHING ★ Bell 14-46; Rice 4-19; Carr 3-27; Aguiar 1-0

LONDON RUSHING ★ J. Alexander 15–33; D. Smith 6-33; Brinson 1-8; Ebubedike 1-3; Horne 1-0; Witkowski 1-(-1)

London Monarchs defensive lineman John Shannon (71) takes to the air to prevent Barcelona Dragons quarterback Tony Rice getting his pass away during the second half of the World Bowl.

THE WORLD LEAGUE OF AMERICAN FOOTBALL 1992

WORLD LEAGUE OF AMERICAN FOOTBALL

New York offices
540 Madison Avenue, New York, NY 10022
Tel: 0101 212 838–9400

Dallas offices
The Waterway Tower, 433 E. Las Colinas Blvd, Suite 100,
Irving, TX 75039. Tel: 0101 214–556–0220

Chairman of the Board Daniel M. Rooney
(President, Pittsburgh Steelers)
Vice-President/Chief Operating Officer
Joseph A. Bailey III
Vice-President/Football Management
Jerome R. Vainisi
Vice-President/Marketing Robert C. Sloane
Vice-President/Communications Bob Rose
Vice-President/European Operations
Dick Regan
European Co-ordinator Bruce Dworshak
Director of Information Vince Casey

WORLD LEAGUE TEAMS

EUROPEAN DIVISION
Barcelona Dragons
Frankfurt Galaxy
London Monarchs

NORTH AMERICAN EAST DIVISION
Montreal Machine
New York-New Jersey Knights
Ohio Glory
Orlando Thunder

NORTH AMERICAN WEST DIVISION
Birmingham Fire
Sacramento Surge
San Antonio Riders

WEEK ONE

SATURDAY, MARCH 21
Birmingham at Sacramento
Frankfurt at Barcelona

SUNDAY, MARCH 22
Ohio at Orlando
Montreal at San Antonio
New York-New Jersey at
London

WEEK TWO

SATURDAY, MARCH 28
Frankfurt at London
New York-New Jersey at
Barcelona
Orlando at Montreal

SUNDAY, MARCH 29
Sacramento at Ohio
San Antonio at Birmingham

WEEK THREE

SATURDAY, APRIL 4
London at Barcelona
Montreal at Sacramento
San Antonio at New York-
New Jersey

SUNDAY, APRIL 5
Birmingham at Frankfurt
Orlando at Ohio

WEEK FOUR

SATURDAY, APRIL 11
Barcelona at Frankfurt
Birmingham at London
San Antonio at Sacramento

SUNDAY, APRIL 12
Ohio at Montreal
New York-New Jersey at
Orlando

WEEK FIVE

SATURDAY, APRIL 18
Barcelona at London
Frankfurt at New York-New
Jersey
Sacramento at Birmingham

SUNDAY, APRIL 19
Ohio at San Antonio
Montreal at Orlando

WEEK SIX

SATURDAY, APRIL 25
Birmingham at San Antonio
Orlando at Frankfurt

SUNDAY, APRIL 26
Ohio at Barcelona
New York-New Jersey at
Montreal
Sacramento at London

WEEK SEVEN

SATURDAY, MAY 2
Barcelona at Birmingham
Frankfurt at Ohio

SUNDAY, MAY 3
London at New York-New
Jersey
Orlando at San Antonio
Sacramento at Montreal

WEEK EIGHT

SATURDAY, MAY 9
Frankfurt at Sacramento
London at Orlando

SUNDAY, MAY 10
Montreal at Birmingham
New York-New Jersey at
Ohio
San Antonio at Barcelona

WEEK NINE

SATURDAY, MAY 16
Barcelona at New York-
New Jersey
Ohio at Sacramento

SUNDAY, MAY 17
London at Montreal
Orlando at Birmingham
San Antonio at Frankfurt

WEEK TEN

SATURDAY, MAY 23
Barcelona at Orlando
Birmingham at Ohio
London at Frankfurt
Montreal at New York-New
Jersey
Sacramento at San Antonio

POST-SEASON GAMES

SATURDAY, MAY 30
Semi-final play-off
(8.00pm EDT; 1.00am
Sunday BST)

SUNDAY, MAY 31
Semi-final play-off (1.00pm
EDT; 6.00pm BST)

SATURDAY, JUNE 6
World Bowl (8.00pm EDT;
1.00am Sunday BST)
Olympic Stadium, Montreal

(Schedule correct at time of
going to press. Dates
subject to change)

STRENGTH OF SCHEDULE			
(Combined 1991 records of teams' 1992 opponents)			
	WON	LOST	PCT
New York-New Jersey	37	23	.617
Orlando	42	28	.600
Barcelona	35	25	.583
Sacramento	29	21	.580
Birmingham	40	30	.571
Frankfurt	39	31	.557
London	37	33	.528
San Antonio	37	33	.528
Montreal	31	29	.517
Ohio	41	39	.512

BARCELONA DRAGONS

Address Estadi Olimpic, Passeig Olimpic, 08004
Barcelona, Catalonia, Spain
Stadium Montjuic Stadium (capacity 70,000)
General Manager Jack Teele
Head Coach Jack Bicknell
Team Colours Dark green, scarlet and gold
1991 record 8–2 (2nd in European Division),
World Bowl runners-up

SCOUTING REPORT   The Barcelona
Dragons will be just as tough to beat in 1992 as they
were last season if they can repeat the sound, solid
football which took them all the way to the World
Bowl. Without being outstanding in any of the
offensive or defensive categories, they were a team
who rarely beat themselves with costly turnovers. At
plus 12, their takeaway/giveaway ratio was the best in
the league – a major reason why they conceded only
126 points during the regular season, second best in
the league, despite having only the fifth best
defensive unit in terms of opposition yardage. No
team ever scored more than 22 points against the
Dragons, and on seven occasions they held their
opponents to 14 points or less.

Offensively, they preferred to rely on the run where
possible, although the production of their rushing
game suffered after Week Four when running back
Paul Palmer (formerly with the Kansas City Chiefs,
Detroit Lions and Dallas Cowboys) suffered a
hamstring injury which halted his fast start to the
season. Jim Bell carried the workload from there on
and despite leading the club in rushing yards his
average gain was a less than impressive 2.7 yards per
carry. In fact, although the rankings show the
Dragons as the third best rushing team for yards
gained, six teams bettered their average gain per

attempt. Close to the goal line the Dragons handed
over responsibility to Lydell Carr, who proved his
effectiveness with eight touchdowns. If coach Jack
Bicknell intends to keep the emphasis on the ground
game this season, he should have been looking in the
draft to supplement his running back corps with a
big-play threat.

The Dragons' passing game was unspectacular but
effective. Scott Erney ended as the second highest
rated quarterback in the league, thanks mainly to
throwing only two interceptions all season – which
made his four-interception performance in the World
Bowl against the London Monarchs all the more
difficult to explain. Erney received pretty good
protection from his offensive line; he and back-up
Tony Rice were sacked only 22 times between them.
The Barcelona offense, ranked fourth overall in the
league, proved one of the more capable units at
producing the big play when required, finishing
second in both third down conversion (36.4 per cent)
and fourth down conversion (53.8). On defense, the
Dragons finished a misleading third in the rankings
against the rush. Although giving up only 80.3 yards
per game, this was largely because teams preferred to
attack a vulnerable secondary. Only two teams
yielded more than the 4.1 yards per carry given up by
Barcelona. Similarly, only two teams allowed
opponents to complete a greater percentage of their
passes than the Dragons. What saved them was their
ability to come up with the drive-killing play (16
interceptions) and put pressure on quarterbacks,
particularly from the defensive ends, where Bruce
Clark and Steve Alvord shared 12 of the club's 33
sacks. Pass defense remains, however, the greatest
area of concern for Bicknell.

As you would expect from a team so strong in the fundamentals of the game, the Dragons' special teams performed efficiently, although they went through the season without returning either a kick-off or punt for a touchdown. Their kick-off coverage was the best in the league, and kicker Massimo Manca was consistent until asked to attempt anything from further than 40 yards.

HEAD COACH Jack Bicknell took up his first professional head coach's position following a successful ten-year tenure at Boston College, where he earned the reputation as one of the leading offensive tacticians in the U.S. His record as head coach at Boston (59–55–1) includes four Bowl appearances, three of them in consecutive years following the 1982, 1983 and 1984 seasons. His most successful campaign was in 1984 when B.C. – led by Heisman Trophy-winning quarterback Doug Flutie – posted a 10–2 record, including a 45–28 Cotton Bowl victory over Houston. He was selected as head coach for two post-season college All-Star games in 1985, the Hula and Japan Bowls, and for the 1990 East-West Shrine Game. Known as Cowboy Jack for his love of country music and horseback riding, Bicknell became a major celebrity during his first season in Barcelona, where the local fans christened him 'El Cabalero'.

Louis Aguiar's punting helped to put the Dragons special teams among the league's best.

PASSING	Att	Cmp	Yds	Cmp%	Yds/Att	TD	TD%	Int	Int%	Lng	Rating
Erney	158	79	1186	50.0	7.51	8	5.1	2	1.3	81t	86.6
Rice	129	69	915	53.5	7.09	1	0.8	3	2.3	57	69.1
Gruden	1	0	0	0	0.00	0	0.0	0	0.0	0	39.6
TEAM	288	148	2101	51.4	7.30	9	3.1	5	1.7	81t	78.5

RUSHING	No	Yds	Avg	Lng	TD
Bell	137	367	2.7	15	0
Palmer	93	358	3.8	22	2
Rice	33	210	6.4	24	2
Henderson*	35	175	5.0	35t	1
Carr	27	89	3.3	24	8
Erney	18	58	3.2	14	1
Woods	1	28	28.0	28t	1
Teeming	3	18	6.0	17	0
Gomez	1	8	8.0	8	0
Taylor	1	–4	–4.0	–4	0
TEAM	314	1132	3.6	28t	14

RECEIVING	No	Yds	Avg	Lng	TD
Taylor	35	745	21.3	81t	6
Davis	34	461	13.6	40	3
Egerton	27	336	12.4	57	0
Woods	20	223	11.2	37	0
Palmer	7	102	14.6	49	0
Hinnant	7	56	8.0	11	0
Henderson*	7	32	4.6	10	0
Bell	6	45	7.5	18	0
Norman	4	63	15.8	28	0
Cherry†	4	37	9.3	10	0
TEAM	148	2101	14.2	81t	9

PUNT RETURNS	Ret	Fc	Yds	Avg	Lng	TD
Egerton	10	4	91	9.1	16	0
Woods	9	3	123	13.7	35	0
TEAM	19	7	214	11.3	35	0

KICK-OFF RETURNS	No	Yds	Avg	Lng	TD
Woods	13	263	20.2	16	0
Palmer	8	151	18.9	27	0
Egerton	4	99	24.8	44	0
Bell	2	37	18.5	21	0
Davis	2	24	12.0	20	0
Cherry†	1	22	22.0	22	0
Greene	1	8	8.0	8	0
Henderson*	1	17	17.0	17	0
TEAM	31	604	19.5	44	0

*Stats for Birmingham and Barcelona
†Not on roster at end of season

INTERCEPTIONS	No	Yds	Avg	Lng	TD
Goetz	4	7	1.8	4	0
Jones	3	43	14.3	35	0
Greene	3	22	7.3	12	0
King†	2	19	9.5	19	0
Fryar	2	13	6.5	12	0
Naposki	1	27	27.0	27t	1
Lindstrom	1	3	3.0	3	0
TEAM	16	134	8.4	35	1

● 1991 RESULTS ●

Mar 24	New York-New Jersey	W	19–7	(19,223)
Apr 1	at Montreal	W	34–10	(53,238)
Apr 6	at Raleigh-Durham	W	26–14	(19,656)
Apr 14	Orlando	W	33–13	(40,875)
Apr 20	at San Antonio	L	14–22	(16,500)
Apr 27	at Sacramento	W	29–20	(19,045)
May 4	Birmingham	W	11–6	(31,490)
May 11	San Antonio	W	17–7	(23,670)
May 19	Frankfurt	L	3–10	(29,753)
May 27	at London	W	20–17	(50,835)

● 1992 SCHEDULE ●

Sat, Mar 21	Frankfurt
Sat, Mar 28	New York-New Jersey
Sat, Apr 4	London
Sat, Apr 11	at Frankfurt
Sat, Apr 18	at London
Sun, Apr 26	Ohio
Sat, May 2	at Birmingham
Sun, May 10	San Antonio
Sat, May 16	at New York-New Jersey
Sat, May 23	at Orlando

SACKS

Clark 7; Naposki 7; Alvord 5; Lindstrom 4; Reese 2.5; White 2; Ruth 1.5; Cobb 1; Goetz 1; Howard 1; Quast 1. **TEAM: 33**

KICKING	FG-19	20-29	30-39	40-49	50+	PAT	Pts
Manca	0/0	9/11	4/5	1/6	0/0	18/21	60

PUNTING	No	Yds	Avg	Net	TB	In20	Lng	Blk
Aguiar	49	2029	41.4	33.8	3	15	80	1

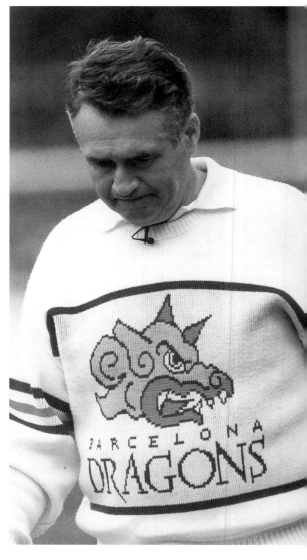

● **Dragons head coach Jack Bicknell is a picture of disappointment at the World Bowl against the London Monarchs.**

BARCELONA DRAGONS roster

No	Name	Pos	Ht	Wt	Born	College	How Acqd
72	Adams, Scott	T	6-5	281	28/9/68	Georgia	D3
12	Aguiar, Louis	P	6-2	200	30/6/66	Utah State	D1
61	Alvord, Steve	DE	6-4	259	2/10/64	Washington	D2
66	Apolskis, Rick	G	6-3	269	6/1/67	Arkansas	D8
22	Bell, Jim	RB	6-1	210	24/6/65	Boston College	D2
63	Brandom, John	C	6-3	282	4/8/66	Arizona	FA
44	Carr, Lydell	RB	6-1	230	27/5/65	Oklahoma	D3
75	Clark, Bruce	DE	6-3	275	31/3/58	Penn State	S4
27	Cobb, Glenn	SS	6-1	212	14/10/66	Illinois	D7
88	Davis, Demetrius	TE	6-0	238	3/1/67	UNLV	D3
82	Egerton, Tim	WR	5-8	164	1/9/68	Delaware State	D4
59	El-Masry, John	LB	6-2	235	25/1/65	Duke	FA
6	Erney, Scott	QB	6-1	206	12/12/66	Rutgers	D1
29	Fryar, Charles	DB	5-10	172	28/11/65	Nebraska	D4
56	Goetz, Ron	LB	6-2	234	8/2/68	Minnesota	D1
35	Gomez, Guillermo	RB	6-1	218	30/6/69	(Spain)	DIS
21	Greene, Anthony	CB	5-8	164	24/6/66	Wake Forest	D1
23	Henderson, Joe	RB	6-1	205	9/4/66	Iowa State	BIR
86	Hinnant, Mike	TE	6-4	225	8/9/66	Temple	D1
53	Howard, Todd	LB	6-3	253	18/2/65	Texas A&M	D6
20	Jones, Adrian	CB	6-0	179	18/1/69	Missouri	D2
2	Johnson, Wayne	QB	6-4	216	13/4/66	Georgia	EA
46	Koulen, Ric	CB	6-1	201	14/5/63	(Netherlands)	DIS
50	Lindstrom, Eric	LB	6-3	230	27/5/66	Boston College	NY
10	Manca, Massimo	K	5-10	191	9/9/64	Penn State	D1
89	Marcos, Xisco	WR	5-11	180	9/5/66	(Spain)	DIS
77	Mickel, Jeff	OL	6-6	307	4/8/66	East Washington	D1
25	Morris, Alex	DB	6-1	185	21/9/65	Texas A&M	D1
57	Mull, Curt	OL	6-4	289	17/4/67	Georgia	D5
26	Palmer, Paul	RB	5-9	184	14/10/65	Temple	D1
91	Naposki, Eric	LB	6-1	248	10/12/68	Connecticut	D4
84	Norman, Dempsey	WR	5-7	175	7/2/66	St Francis	FA
78	Pearce, Mark	DE	6-7	255	10/4/67	(England)	DIS
55	Quast, Brad	LB	6-2	246	5/6/68	Iowa	D2
92	Reese, Jerry	NT	6-1	282	11/7/64	Kentucky	D4
4	Rice, Tony	QB	6-0	185	5/9/67	Notre Dame	D2
62	Ruth, Mike	NT	6-2	266	25/6/64	Boston	S1
52	Sign, Bobby	C	6-2	287	23/5/66	Baylor	NFL
80	Taylor, Gene	WR	6-2	189	12/11/62	Fresno State	D1
33	Teeming, Frank	RB	6-0	200	23/4/70	(Netherlands)	DIS
60	Voorhees, Barry	G	6-4	289	7/12/63	Cal State, Northridge	D6
96	White, Brent	DE	6-4	268	28/2/67	Michigan	D1
85	Woods, Thomas	WR	5-10	182	21/2/67	Tennessee	D2

Roster correct at end of 1991 season. Key to How Acquired column: D1 – first round draft pick; S1 – first round pick in supplementary draft; FA – free agent; DIS – Operation Discovery; NY – formerly with New York-New Jersey; BIR – formerly with Birmingham; EA – extra allocation draft; NFL – NFL enhancement allocation.

BIRMINGHAM FIRE

Address Financial Center Offices, 925 Financial
Center, 505 North 20th Street, Birmingham,
Alabama 35203
Stadium Legion Field (capacity 72,000)
General Manager Position vacant at time of writing
Head Coach Chan Gailey
Team Colours Navy blue, gold and crimson
1991 record 5–5 (North American West Division
champions), beaten in semi-final play-offs

SCOUTING REPORT Birmingham Fire won their
division and reached the semi-final play-offs in 1991,
which was as far as their big-play defense could carry
them. If they are to better, or even match, that
achievement this season, their offense is going to
have to start shouldering some of the burden. After
losing three of their first four games, the Fire defense
helped the team go 4–2 in the final six games by
never conceding more than 14 points. In contrast,
Birmingham's miserable offense could total only 24
points in the club's five defeats. The main reason for
their division championship can be found in the
turnover column. They took the ball away from their
opponents 37 times during the season for a ratio of
plus eleven. It helped, of coure, that the Fire were in
the weakest of the league's three divisions, although
they can justifiably claim to be the best of the U.S.
teams after posting a 5–0 record against teams from
their own country. It was a different story against the
European and Canadian sides. They went 0–6,
including their semi-final defeat against Barcelona.
A familiar story unfolded in that match, with the
defense performing heroically while the offense cost
them the game by committing six turnovers in a 10–3
defeat in front of their fans.

It would be easy to lay the blame for the Fire's

offensive failures at the feet, and arm, of quarterback
Brent Pease. Maybe that is too convenient a way to
explain why Birmingham were the bottom-ranked
unit in the league, but it is certainly a good place to
start. The first quarterback selected in the league
draft, Pease was earmarked as a likely star of the
inaugural season. By the end of the year he had
completed only 46.7 per cent of his passes for a
paltry five touchdowns. He had also failed completely
to provide Birmingham with the leadership they
expected of a man with three years of NFL experience
with the Houston Oilers behind him. Pease was
booed consistently by the Legion Field fans, who saw
the starting job for the semi-final game go to Eric
Jones, who could hardly claim to have earned the
honour with one touchdown pass, nine interceptions
and a pathetic rating of 29.3. Clearly, the
quarterback position should have been the number
one priority for head coach Chan Gailey going into
this season's draft. Both the passing game and
rushing game ranked ninth in the league, with the
Fire's average ground gain of 3.3 yards tying the
Raleigh-Durham Skyhawks for last place. The
acquisition of Elroy Harris off waivers from Montreal
failed to provide them with the feature back they
desperately need. There were plenty of worse
offensive lines around the league than Birmingham,
who gave up only 19 sacks during the season, a figure
bettered only by the London Monarchs.

Against the pass, the Fire defense ranked only
sixth in the league, but it was the predatory instincts
of their secondary which made them such a force.
Their backfield featured All-World League free safety
John Miller (six interceptions), strong safety Arthur
Hunter (six interceptions) and All-World League

cond-team cornerback John Holland, all of whom lped their club equal New York-New Jersey's total 21 interceptions. Up front, Birmingham applied ly modest pressure to opposing quarterbacks, cording 25 sacks. The dangers in trying to pass ainst the Fire defense meant that teams resorted ore to the running game, leaving Birmingham nked as low as seventh in yards allowed. But with iddle linebacker John Brantley an imposing force – e earned a third share of the Defensive MVP award they surrendered just 3.7 yards per play, tying for cond best in the league.

On special teams, Birmingham featured some of e best coverage in the league, never allowing a punt kick-off to be returned for a touchdown, and asted one of the best punters in Kirk Maggio. They

will hope to improve their kicking following Win Lyle's failure to convert more than three of his seven field goal attempts from beyond 30 yards, despite a perfect record on extra points.

HEAD COACH Chan Gailey came to national prominence in the U.S. as a member of the coaching staff which helped the Denver Broncos to three Super Bowl appearances in the late 1980s. He graduated from tight ends and special teams coach in 1986 and 1987 to quarterback coach in 1988 and offensive co-ordinator/wide receivers coach in 1989. Gailey's first head coaching position was at Troy State University in 1983 and 1984, when he led the Trojans to the NCAA Division II National Championship and was named Division II Coach of the Year.

The Fire offense was e league's poorest.

PASSING	Att	Cmp	Yds	Cmp%	Yds/Att	TD	TD%	Int	Int%	Lng	Rating
Pease	182	85	922	46.7	5.07	5	2.7	6	3.3	87t	57.5
Jones	87	41	495	47.1	5.69	1	1.1	9	10.3	42t	29.3
Maggio	2	1	65	50.0	32.50	1	50.0	0	0.0	65t	135.4
Mobley	1	1	15	100.0	15.00	1	100.0	0	0.0	15t	158.3
TEAM	271	128	1497	47.1	5.50	8	2.9	15	5.5	87t	51.1

RUSHING	No	Yds	Avg	Lng	TD
Harris*	135	540	4.0	41t	3
Bell	66	192	2.9	11	1
Henderson†	35	175	5.0	35t	1
Avery	25	102	4.1	23	1
Pease	27	79	2.9	11	0
Jones	15	30	2.0	11	0
Mobley	7	27	3.9	15	1
Wilson†	2	10	5.0	7	0
McGowan	2	6	3.0	3	0
Maggio	4	-46	-11.5	0	0
TEAM	261	865	3.3	35t	4

RECEIVING	No	Yds	Avg	Lng	TD
Bell	40	347	8.7	65t	1
Bouyer	28	465	16.3	87t	2
Avery	17	197	11.6	32t	2
Ross	12	129	10.8	21	0
Mobley	8	154	19.3	55t	2
Harris*	8	29	3.6	9	0
Henderson†	7	32	4.6	10	0
Hopkins	6	86	14.3	25	0
Wilson†	3	28	9.3	17	0
Newsom	3	12	4.0	5	0
Motzkus	2	37	18.5	28	0
Pease	1	15	15.0	15t	1
TEAM	128	1497	11.7	87t	8

INTERCEPTIONS	No	Yds	Avg	Lng	TD
Miller	6	93	32.2	99t	1
Hunter	6	72	12.0	37t	1
Holland	3	38	12.7	17	0
Henry	2	83	41.5	77t	1
Gage	2	15	7.5	15	0
McGowan	1	12	12.0	12	0
Sanders	1	0	0.0	0	0
TEAM	21	143	19.7	99t	3

*Stats for Montreal and Birmingham
†Not on roster at end of season

PUNT RETURNS	Ret	Fc	Yds	Avg	Lng	TD
Henry	23	5	247	10.7	73	1
Mobley	3	0	98	32.7	64	0
TEAM	26	5	345	13.3	73	1

KICK-OFF RETURNS	No	Yds	Avg	Lng	TD
Wilson†	12	218	18.2	29	0
Bell	8	197	24.6	28	0
Henry	7	147	21.0	49	0
Thorson	2	7	3.5	7	0
Harris	1	25	25.0	25	0
Henderson†	1	17	17.0	17	0
Hopkins	1	0	0.0	0	0
Mobley	1	15	15.0	15	0
TEAM	33	626	19.0	49	0

● 1991 RESULTS ●

Mar 23	Montreal	L	5–20	(53,000)
Mar 30	Sacramento	W	17–10	(16,500)
Apr 8	at Montreal	L	10–23	(27,766)
Apr 15	London	L	0–27	(18,500)
Apr 21	at Orlando	W	31–6	(21,249)
Apr 29	San Antonio	W	16–12	(8,000)
May 4	at Barcelona	L	6–11	(31,490)
May 12	at Frankfurt	L	3–10	(28,127)
May 20	New York-New Jersey	W	24–14	(31,500)
May 25	at Raleigh-Durham	W	28–7	(16,335)

SACKS

Oliver 7; McDaniels 4; Brantley 3; Hyche 3; Jackson 2;
Moore 2; Phillips 2; Bowick 1; McGowan 1. **TEAM: 25**

KICKING	FG1-19	20-29	30-39	40-49	50+	PAT	Pts
Lyle	0/0	2/3	2/4	1/3	0/0	15/15	30

PUNTING	No	Yds	Avg	Net	TB	In20	Lng	Blk
Maggio	61	2558	41.9	36.0	7	19	57	0

● 1992 SCHEDULE ●

Sat, Mar 21	at Sacramento
Sun, Mar 29	San Antonio
Sun, Apr 5	at Frankfurt
Sat, Apr 11	at London
Sat, Apr 18	Sacramento
Sat, Apr 25	at San Antonio
Sat, May 2	Barcelona
Sun, May 10	Montreal
Sat, May 17	Orlando
Sat, May 23	at Ohio

BIRMINGHAM FIRE
roster

No	Name	Pos	Ht	Wt	Born	College	How Acqd
98	Alyson, Gareth	DL	6-4	260	17/5/65	(England)	DIS
50	Anderson, Bill	C	6-3	265	10/8/66	Iowa	D1
42	Avery, Steven	FB	6-2	230	18/8/66	Northern Michigan	D3
41	Bell, Ken	RB	5-11	194	16/11/64	Boston College	FA
80	Bouyer, Willie	WR	6-2	196	24/9/66	Michigan State	D1
70	Bowick, Tony	NT	6-2	284	3/10/66	Tennessee	D2
54	Brantley, John	LB	6-2	243	23/10/65	Georgia	D2
99	Cockrell, Randy	LB	6-1	235	13/6/67	Virginia Tech	D8
48	Gage, Steven	S	6-3	209	10/5/64	Tulsa	R-D
31	Harris, Elroy	RB	5-9	226	18/8/66	Eastern Kentucky	MON
45	Henry, James	CB	5-9	196	24/10/65	Southern Mississippi	D8
21	Holland, John	CB	5-10	186	18/7/65	Cal State, Sacramento	D4
87	Hopkins, Mark	TE	6-3	221	9/3/67	Central Michigan	D2
24	Hunter, Arthur	S	5-11	193	24/1/67	Central State Ohio	D10
56	Hyche, Steve	LB	6-1	236	12/6/63	Livingston	D4
51	Jackson, Junior	LB	5-11	240	31/10/68	Tennessee	D1
7	Jones, Eric	QB	6-1	213	22/6/66	Vanderbilt	D3
73	King, Buddy	T	6-6	264	11/9/67	Southern Mississippi	D4
1	Lyle, Win	K	5-9	180	13/3/68	Auburn	D1
8	Maggio, Kirk	P	5-11	152	19/9/67	UCLA	D7
77	McDaniels, Pellom	DE	6-3	272	21/2/68	Oregon State	D5
53	McGowan, Paul	LB	6-0	222	13/1/66	Florida	D1
44	Miller, John	S	6-1	187	22/6/66	Michigan State	D5
83	Mobley, Stacey	WR	5-8	159	15/9/65	Jackson State	S2
71	Moore, Otis	DE	6-3	272	26/4/64	Clemson	D3
86	Motzkus, Andreas	WR	6-2	193	22/7/67	(Germany)	DIS
79	Mullin, R.C.	T	6-6	315	28/6/65	Southwestern Louisiana	D2
81	Mutti, Paolo	WR	6-1	190	9/1/64	(Italy)	DIS
29	Newsom, Anthony	WR	5-7	172	20/7/65	Stephen F. Austin	D1
76	Odiorne, Charles	G	6-4	275	17/8/67	Texas Tech	D7
59	Oliver, Maurice	LB	6-3	232	14/6/67	Southern Mississippi	D3
10	Pease, Brent	QB	6-2	203	8/10/64	Montana	D1
62	Phillips, Darrell	NT	6-0	256	9/3/65	Louisiana State	D1
84	Riecke, Hans-Ulrich	WR	5-11	196	3/10/63	(Germany)	DIS
82	Ross, Phil	TE	6-3	234	14/6/67	Oregon State	D1
27	Sanders, Tracy	CB	5-11	176	16/5/66	Florida State	D2
75	Schonewolf, Rich	T	6-4	294	19/12/66	Penn State	D8
65	Tanks, Michael	G	6-1	277	4/8/67	Florida State	D9
55	Thorson, Chad	LB	6-2	247	6/7/67	Wheaton College	D6
88	Vissa, Sergio	TE	6-4	270	4/6/68	(Italy)	DIS
52	Yniguez, Paul	G	6-2	279	21/11/67	Kansas State	D6

Roster correct at end of 1991 season. Key to How Acquired column: D1 – first round draft pick; S2 – second round pick in supplementary draft; FA – free agent; DIS – Operation Discovery; R-D – formerly with Raleigh-Durham; MON – formerly with Montreal

FRANKFURT GALAXY

Address Escherscheimer LandStr. 526, 6000
Frankfurt 50, Germany
Stadium Waldstadion (capacity 37,000)
General Manager Oliver Luck
Head Coach Jack Elway
Team Colours Purple, orange and red
1991 record 7–3 (3rd in European Division)

SCOUTING REPORT Beyond a doubt, Frankfurt
Galaxy were one of the World League's top four teams
in 1991. Their failure to underline that status by
qualifying for the semi-final play-offs was due to their
self-destruction in the final game of the season
against Sacramento. A win would have placed Galaxy
second in the European division. Instead, they
committed six turnovers, leaving Frankfurt with a
takeaway/giveaway ratio of minus eleven – the second
worst in the league. Change that statistic this season,
and there is every reason to expect them to be one of
the strongest challengers for London's crown. Add to
this Galaxy's league-leading defense – which helped
to win five games by a touchdown or less – and the
Monarchs could be seriously threatened. In fact,
Frankfurt never won a game by more than 10 points.

To improve their offensive output this season
Frankfurt probably need to provide some support for
running back Tony Baker, with whom their gameplan
started and finished. Their ground game consisted of
Baker left, Baker right and Baker up the middle. The
predictability left the ex-Cleveland Browns and
Phoenix Cardinals rusher with only a 3.3 yard
average gain. While Baker carried the ball 199 times,
the next most frequently used running back was
Harry Jackson, who got his hands around the ball on
just 17 occasions. Baker was also the favourite target
of quarterback Mike Perez, despite a solid season by

Jason Johnson, the pick of the Galaxy wide receivers
Perez was something of an enigma. In some games h
performed superbly, but with the season on the line
against Sacramento he threw four interceptions, and
in his team's early season defeat against the same
opposition he connected on a measly 18 of 48
attempts. No quarterback threw the ball more often
than Perez, and no one was intercepted more often,
his 17 pick-offs outweighing 13 touchdowns.

The key to overpowering the Galaxy defense in
1991 would have been to have gained mastery of the
defensive line. It was a task which proved beyond
just about everyone and the league's head coaches
admitted as much by voting defensive end Mark Mr
and nose tackle Mike Teeter to the All-World Leagu
squad. Their presence helped the Galaxy restrict
opponents to a league-low 3.3 yards per rush. In
addition, the Frankfurt pass rush produced 42 sacks
the third best total of the season, and kept harrassed
quarterbacks down to a 46.7 completion percentage
for an average of 153.9 yards per game, another
league low.

While Jack Elway, known for his wide-open
offense, proved he could coach sound defense as
well, his special teams were somewhat disappointin
Averaging a meagre 3.7 yards on punt returns and
failing ever to run back a kick-off more than 34
yards, the Galaxy were also one of the league's
weaker coverage units. Meanwhile, punter Tom
Whelihan was overshadowed by most of his peers a
the Galaxy were lumbered with one of the most
inaccurate kicking teams in the league. Whelihan
and German kicker Stephan Maslo conspired to mis
five out of seven field goals in the 20–29 yard range
and hit on only two out of six above 40 yards.

HEAD COACH Jack Elway, father of the Denver Broncos' All-Pro quarterback John Elway, established himself as one of America's leading college coaches before taking the Galaxy job. He served as head coach at Cal State-Northridge from 1976 to 1978 before spending five seasons in charge of a San Jose State team which, in 1979 and 1981, earned Top 20 rankings and won the Pacific Coast Athletic Association championship. More success followed during his five years as head coach at Stanford, the school from which his son had just graduated. In 1986 Stanford gained a berth in the Gator Bowl and earned Elway another Top 20 position. A former quarterback at Washington State University, he has been given head coaching assignments in two college All-Star games, the Blue-Gray Game and the East-West Shrine Game. Interestingly, Elway was set to coach London Lightning in the International League of American Football in the spring of 1990, when the league collapsed without ever reaching opening day, never to reappear on the scene.

Kevin Hendrix tackles London's David Smith.

PASSING	Att	Cmp	Yds	Cmp%	Yds/Att	TD	TD%	Int	Int%	Lng	Rating
Perez	357	171	2272	47.9	6.36	13	3.6	17	4.8	59	60.8
Whelihan	1	0	0	00.0	0.00	0	0.0	1	100.0	0	0.0
TEAM	358	171	2272	47.8	6.38	13	3.6	18	5.0	59	59.5

RUSHING	No	Yds	Avg	Lng	TD
Baker	199	648	3.3	26	5
Perez	44	189	4.3	26	0
Jackson	17	61	3.6	14	0
Whelihan	2	7	3.5	7	0
Bartalo	1	0	0.0	0	0
McCree	3	–4	–1.3	1	0
Lee	1	–5	–5.0	–5	0
TEAM	267	896	3.4	26	5

SACKS

Alexander 7; Mraz 6.5; Williams 6.5; Hendrix 4; Broady 3.5; Wolfolk 3.5; Teeter 3; Moorer 2.5; Pau'u 2.5; Fleming† 1; Gatlin 1; Seals 1. **TEAM: 42**

KICKING	FG1-19	20-29	30-29	40-49	50+	PAT	Pts
Maslo	0/0	1/3	3/5	2/5	0/0	7/9	25
Whelihan	1/1	1/4	2/2	0/1	0/0	6/7	18
TEAM	1/1	2/7	5/7	2/6	0/0	13/16	43

PUNTING	No	Yds	Avg	Net	TB	In20	Lng	Blk
Whelihan	49	1846	37.7	32.9	2	18	61	0

†Not on roster at end of season

RECEIVING	No	Yds	Avg	Lng	TD
Baker	39	423	10.8	28	1
Johnson	38	635	16.7	59	4
Gordon	22	289	13.1	36t	3
Lee	21	308	14.7	29	0
Fortune	20	215	10.8	24	1
Morton	17	264	15.5	36t	2
Bartalo	9	102	11.3	28	1
Young	3	27	9.0	17	1
Jackson	1	9	9.0	9	0
McCree	1	0	0.0	0	0
TEAM	171	2272	13.3	59	13

● 1991 RESULTS ●

Mar 23	London	L	11–24	(23,169)
Apr 1	at San Antonio	W	10–3	(18,432)
Apr 6	at New York-New Jersey	W	27–17	(36,546)
Apr 13	at Sacramento	L	10–16	(17,065)
Apr 20	Raleigh-Durham	W	30–28	(21,065)
Apr 27	Montreal	W	17–7	(25,269)
May 4	at Orlando	W	17–14	(11,270)
May 12	Birmingham	W	10–3	(28,127)
May 19	at Barcelona	W	10–3	(29,753)
May 25	Sacramento	L	13–24	(51,653)

● 1992 SCHEDULE ●

Sat, Mar 21	at Barcelona
Sat, Mar 28	at London
Sun, Apr 5	Birmingham
Sat, Apr 11	Barcelona
Sat, Apr 18	at New York-New Jersey
Sat, Apr 25	Orlando
Sat, May 2	at Ohio
Sat, May 9	at Sacramento
Sun, May 17	San Antonio
Sat, May 23	London

INTERCEPTIONS	No	Yds	Avg	Lng	TD
Stallworth	3	38	12.7	38	0
Finch	2	21	10.5	21	0
Greenwood	2	9	4.5	9	0
Broady	2	4	2.0	4	0
Seals	1	27	27.0	27	0
Johnson	1	17	17.0	17	0
TEAM	11	116	10.5	38	0

KICK-OFF RETURNS	No	Yds	Avg	Lng	TD
Baker	14	296	21.1	34	0
Gordon	10	187	18.7	29	0
Johnson	4	85	21.3	26	0
Bartalo	2	3	1.5	3	0
Jackson	1	11	11.0	11	0
TEAM	31	582	18.8	34	0

PUNT RETURNS	Ret	Fc	Yds	Avg	Lng	TD
Johnson	24	16	89	3.7	15	0

FRANKFURT GALAXY roster

No	Name	Pos	Ht	Wt	Born	College	How Acqd
50	Alexander, Chris	LB	6-0	214	9/6/65	San Jose State	S4
33	Baker, Tony	RB	5-9	185	11/6/64	East Carolina	D1
25	Bartalo, Steve	FB	5-8	187	15/7/64	Colorado	D4
28	Broady, Timothy	S	5-11	213	20/2/66	Murray State	D7
89	Craig, Keith	WR	6-0	175	29/11/67	(Germany)	DIS
63	Diaz-Infante, David	G	6-2	278	31/3/64	San Jose	D3
14	Espinoza, Alex	QB	6-0	203	31/5/64	Iowa State	D3
20	Finch, Lonnie	CB	6-0	174	12/10/66	Mississippi Col.	D6
81	Fortune, Chad	TE	6-3	235	13/8/67	Louisville	D7
65	Frank, Garry	G	6-2	292	20/12/64	Mississippi State	D1
	Gatlin, Todd	LB	6-2	238	7/8/66	Florida	SAC
88	Gordon, Cedric	WR	5-10	181	6/11/66	Ferris State	D5
46	Greenwood, Joe	CB	5-11	186	8/7/66	Temple	D10
75	Hackemack, Ken	T	6-9	309	20/9/67	Texas	D8
70	Hampel, Olaf	NT	6-6	280	24/6/67	(Germany)	DIS
78	Hendrix, Kevin	DE	6-2	269	21/1/66	South Carolina	D3
62	Huckestein, Ray	NT	6-1	278	22/1/67	Stanford	D7
45	Jackson, Harry	RB	5-10	228	15/3/68	St Cloud State	D2
87	Johnson, Jason	WR	5-10	178	8/11/65	Illinois State	S3
90	Jones, Lee	DE	6-0	265	24/10/64	Nebraska	D6
89	Lee, Alvin	WR	5-10	196	6/12/67	Louisiana State	D8
7	Maslo, Stephan	K	5-11	185	5/1/64	(Germany)	DIS
40	McCoy, Keith	CB	5-10	193	27/11/64	Fresno State	D2
31	McCree, Charles	CB	5-11	192	29/12/66	Minnesota	D11
55	Moorer, Pat	LB	6-0	237	20/6/68	Florida	D2
86	Morton, Craig	WR	6-0	166	4/5/67	Dartmouth	D6
60	Mounts, Rod	G	6-3	280	27/7/65	Texas A&I	D6
72	Mraz, Mark	DE	6-3	257	9/2/65	Utah State	D2
77	Olszewski, Gerald	G	6-4	250	28/7/66	(Germany)	DIS
57	Pau'u, Yepi	LB	6-0	220	28/4/65	San Jose State	D2
11	Perez, Mike	QB	6-1	211	7/3/63	San Jose State	D1
67	Poe, Billy	G	6-2	296	26/4/64	Moorhead State	D9
22	Seals, Mark	S	6-1	201	31/1/67	Boston	D6
27	Stallworth, Cedric	CB	5-10	182	31/3/67	Georgia Tech	D1
58	Still, Eric	G	6-2	279	28/6/67	Tennessee	D4
76	Teeter, Mike	NT	6-2	266	4/10/67	Michigan	D1
1	Whelihan, Tom	K/P	5-9	204	15/8/66	Missouri	D1
96	Williams, Chris	NT	6-3	304	23/11/68	American Int.	D5
50	Wolfolk, Kevin	LB	6-1	234	6/2/67	Portland State	D3
80	Young, Todd	WR	6-6	257	2/2/67	Penn State	D2

Roster correct at end of 1991 season. Key to How Acquired column: D1 — first round draft pick; S3 — third round pick in supplementary draft; DIS — Operation Discovery; SAC — formerly with Sacramento

LONDON MONARCHS

Address Uncertain at time of writing
Stadium Wembley Stadium (capacity 63,500)
General Manager Billy Hicks
Head Coach Larry Kennan
Team Colours Royal blue, metallic gold and red
1991 record 9–1 (European Division champions),
World Bowl winners

SCOUTING REPORT More of the same, please,
will be the message from their fans as head coach
Larry Kennan and his team set about defending their
World League crown. If the same mixture of explosive
offense, intimidating defense, astute coaching, and
excellent team chemistry is present this season, the
Monarchs stand every chance of achieving the feat
which has historically proved so difficult in this sport
repeating as champions.

The only winning ingredient they may not be able
to recreate is the tide of emotion which swept them to
their triumph last year, overcoming the obstacles of
being thousands of miles from home, living and
training in spartan conditions and preparing for
games with the weariness of trans-Atlantic travel still
in their bones. Despite these disadvantages, the
longer the 1991 season went on, the more it appeared
that the Monarchs were destined to lift the World
Bowl trophy in front of their Wembley fans.

London Monarchs safety Dedrick Dodge dives into the end zone to score the decisive touchdown against the New York-New Jersey Knights in Week Eight.

The Monarchs offense and defense, ranked first and second in the league respectively, did plenty to give fate a helping hand, however. Their one defeat came in the final, meaningless game of the regular season on the only occasion they failed to amass 22 points – a target their opponents fell short of in every game. Top points scorers in the league, the Monarchs offense was built on the solid foundations of their passing game, with quarterback Stan Gelbaugh proving himself without peer among World League play-callers. With the protection of the best offensive line in the league, who allowed just 10 sacks, he took advantage of probably the most complete set of receivers to finish top in virtually every category in which a quarterback can be judged. There are no statistics to gauge leadership and temperament, but one look at Gelbaugh commanding his troops was more eloquent than any amount of numbers and percentages. Gelbaugh's NFL achievements since last June may rob the Monarchs of his services in 1992; if this is the case, Kennan, a great evaluator of talent, can be relied upon to have shopped wisely in the draft – either for a new starter or a back-up to John Witkowski, who is too good and experienced to be sitting on World League benches.

Running back Judd Garrett's soft hands provided the launch pad for the long bombs which made Jon Horton the league's leading receiver in terms of yardage. Andre Riley brought his toughness and great moves to a passing game which topped the league at 281.5 yards per game. The Monarchs had no need of a great running game, but finished with a decent enough 4.2 yard average gain, while the effectiveness of their ground attack close to the goal line was shown by their 17 rushing touchdowns. London could certainly benefit, however, from the acquisition of a back with game-breaking potential.

Defensively, the Monarchs were fearsome against the rush, yielding only 3.7 yards at a time. The presence of nose tackle Roy Hart anchoring the defensive line was a major factor, just as it was in restricting opposing quarterbacks to a 47.5 completion percentage. No team put more pressure on the passer, and Hart, with lightning quick feet for such a big man, and outside linebacker Danny Lockett, a human fireball, shared almost half the club's league-leading 53 sacks. Strength at the defensive ends and a consistent linebacking corps added considerable support.

Dana Brinson was one of the league's most dangerous return men, but penalties hindered his efforts on more than one occasion. The Monarchs were, in fact, the most penalised team in 1991; a repeat of this in 1992 could be costly if their games are closer. The jury is still out on British kicker Phil Alexander, who made the All-World League team but never had to perform with the game on the line. The punting game needs improvement; Greg Horne finished with a low average, too many blocks and not enough kicks inside the opponents' 20-yard line.

HEAD COACH Larry Kennan, a quarterback at LaVerne College, became a head coach for the first time in 1979 at Lamar University, Texas, where he spent three years before joining the Los Angeles Raiders' coaching staff for a six-year stint. Having won a Super Bowl ring following the 1983 season, he enjoyed a year as quarterback coach of the Denver Broncos, working with John Elway. He then spent two years as offensive coordinator of the Indianapolis Colts, from whom he was hired by the Monarchs. Born in California in June 1944, he has now logged 26 years of coaching experience.

RUSHING	No	Yds	Avg	Lng	TD
Alexander, J.	87	391	4.5	41t	9
Smith, D.	84	302	3.6	28t	6
Garrett	23	75	3.3	15	0
Gelbaugh	9	66	7.3	48	0
Ebubedike	12	64	5.3	18	1
Brinson	4	47	11.8	23	1
Flannigan	10†	29	2.9	9	0
Riley	1	22	22.0	22	0
Witkowski	6	–5	–0.8	1	0
TEAM	236	991	4.2	1	17

INTERCEPTIONS	No	Yds	Avg	Lng	TD
Dodge	6	202	33.7	62	2
Ervin	2	13	6.5	13	0
Smith, I.	2	8	4.0	8	0
Crossman	1	29	29.0	29	0
Robertson	1	12	12.0	12	0
Sale	1	8	8.0	8	0
TEAM	13	272	20.9	62	2

PASSING	Att	Cmp	Yds	Cmp%	Yds/Att	TD	TD%	Int	Int%	Lng	Rating
Gelbaugh	303	189	2655	62.4	8.76	17	5.6	12	4.0	96t	92.8
Witkowski	40	23	232	57.5	5.80	2	5.0	2	5.0	28	70.0
TEAM	343	212	2887	61.8	8.42	19	5.5	14	4.1	96t	90.1

RECEIVING	No	Yds	Avg	Lng	TD
Garrett	71	620	8.7	47	1
Horton	43	931	21.7	96t	8
Riley	30	506	16.9	62t	4
Brinson	28	351	12.5	38	1
Sargent	20	316	15.8	38t	4
Alexander, J.	12	91	7.6	23	1
Davis	5	49	9.8	18	0
Smith, D.	2	19	9.5	20	0
Harbour	1	4	4.0	4	0
TEAM	212	2887	13.6	96t	19

KICK-OFF RETURNS	No	Yds	Avg	Lng	TD
Brinson	12	317	26.4	93t	1
Flannigan*†	8	121	15.1	23	0
Garrett	5	92	18.4	23	0
Riley	2	33	16.5	22	0
Alexander, J.	1	0	0.0	0	0
Wilson	1	18	18.0	18	0
TEAM	26	532	20.5	93t	1

*Stats for Orlando and London
†Not on roster at end of season

PUNT RETURNS	Ret	Fc	Yds	Avg	Lng	TD
Brinson	31	3	181	5.8	24	0
Riley	3	1	7	2.3	5	0
TEAM	34	4	188	5.5	24	0

SACKS

Lockett 13.5; Hart 10.5; Brown 7.5; Renna 6.5; Shannon 4; Williams 4; Smith, C. 2.5; Sale 2.5; Robertson 1; Wilson 1

KICKING	FG1-19	20-29	30-39	40-49	50+	PAT	Pts
Alexander, P.	0/0	6/6	2/5	1/2	0/0	37/39	64

PUNTING	No	Yds	Avg	Net	TB	In20	Lng	Blk
Horne	37	1432	38.7	30.2	4	11	56	4

● 1991 RESULTS ●

Mar 23	at Frankfurt	W	24–11	(23,169)
Mar 31	New York-New Jersey	W	22–18	(46,952)
Apr 6	Orlando	W	35–12	(35,327)
Apr 15	at Birmingham	W	27–0	(18,500)
Apr 20	Montreal	W	45–7	(35,294)
Apr 28	Raleigh-Durham	W	35–10	(33,997)
May 6	at San Antonio	W	38–15	(12,328)
May 11	at New York-New Jersey	W	22–7	(41,219)
May 18	at Sacramento	W	45–21	(21,409)
May 27	Barcelona	L	17–20	(50,835)

● 1992 SCHEDULE ●

Sun, Mar 22	New York-New Jersey
Sat, Mar 28	Frankfurt
Sat, Apr 4	at Barcelona
Sat, Apr 11	Birmingham
Sat, Apr 18	Barcelona
Sun, Apr 26	Sacramento
Sun, May 3	at New York-New Jersey
Sat, May 9	at Orlando
Sun, May 17	at Montreal
Sat, May 23	at Frankfurt

● **Monarchs head coach Larry Kennan.**

LONDON MONARCHS roster

No	Name	Pos	Ht	Wt	Born	College	How Acqd
60	Adams, Theo	T	6-4	282	24/4/66	Hawaii	D2
20	Alexander, Jeff	RB	6-1	245	15/1/65	Southern	D1
3	Alexander, Phil	K	6-2	216	4/9/62	(England)	DIS
70	Berardelli, Paul	G	6-2	280	19/11/67	Villanova	D4
81	Brinson, Dana	WR	5-9	165	10/4/65	Nebraska	D1
53	Brown, Marlon	LB	6-3	235	30/7/62	Memphis State	D1
73	Caldwell, David	NT	6-1	261	28/2/65	Texas Christian	FA
44	Carthy, Trevor	CB	5-6	190	27/3/64	(England)	DIS
31	Crossman, Dan	S	6-0	193	17/1/67	Pittsburgh	D6
5	Dahlquist, Eric	QB	6-4	215	12/9/66	Kenyon State	EA
87	Davis, Pat	TE	6-3	280	13/6/66	Syracuse	D1
33	Dodge, Dedrick	S	6-2	184	14/6/67	Florida State	D4
29*	Ebubedike, Victor	RB	6-0	216	1/2/66	(England)	DIS
27	Ervin, Corris	CB	5-11	183	30/8/66	Central Florida	D1
25	Feggins, Howard	CB	5-9	206	6/5/65	North Carolina	D3
52	Foster, Russell	LB	6-0	219	10/9/66	Western Kentucky	S4
64	Fruhmorgen, John	C	6-4	288	28/9/65	Alabama	D5
67	Gabbard, Steve	T	6-3	293	19/7/66	Florida State	D1
22	Garrett, Judd	RB	6-2	208	25/7/67	Princeton	D2
10	Gelbaugh, Stan	QB	6-3	207	4/12/62	Maryland	S1
83	Harbour, David	TE	6-2	268	23/10/65	Illinois	D2
75	Hart, Roy	NT	6-0	293	10/7/65	South Carolina	D1
4	Horne, Greg	P	6-0	179	22/11/64	Arkansas	D1
86	Horton, Jon	WR	6-1	196	26/12/64	Arizona	D2
99	Hoyte, Nigel	DT	6-3	265	16/7/64	(England)	DIS
68	Jones, Larry	G	6-3	290	3/3/67	Hawaii	FA
94	Lockett, Danny	LB	6-3	255	11/7/64	Arizona	D2
59	Marrone, Doug	C	6-4	302	25/7/64	Syracuse	D3
72	Oberdorf, Todd	T	6-6	295	21/1/67	Indiana	D8
95	Renna, Mike	DE	6-4	273	26/7/67	Delaware	D3
80	Riley, Andre	WR	5-9	176	2/12/66	Washington	S2
55	Robertson, Virgil	LB	6-2	226	9/11/66	Nicholls State	FRA
51	Sale, Ken	LB	6-1	222	3/5/68	Texas El Paso	D3
85	Sargent, Tony	WR	5-8	165	1/12/65	Wyoming	FA
71	Shannon, John	DE	6-3	265	18/1/65	Kentucky	D2
54	Singletary, James	LB	6-3	236	17/8/66	East Carolina	D4
90	Smith, Carnel	DE	6-1	271	13/11/66	Pittsburgh	D5
32	Smith, David	RB	6-1	221	3/11/65	Western Kentucky	S3
21	Smith, Irvin	CB	5-10	183	12/3/67	Maryland	D2
56	Williams, Rickey	LB	5-11	227	24/9/65	Arkansas	D7
42	Wilson, Harvey	S	6-1	200	13/12/68	Southern	D5
12	Witkowski, John	QB	6-1	221	18/6/62	Columbia	D1

Roster correct at end of 1991 season. Key to How Acquired column: D1 – first round draft pick; S1 – first round pick in supplementary draft; FA – free agent; DIS – Operation Discovery; EA – extra allowance draft; FRA – formerly with Frankfurt.

*Ebubedike wore number 29 in 11 games, but wore number 36 in the World Bowl.

MONTREAL MACHINE

Address 4551 Pierre-de-Coubertin, Montreal (Quebec) HIV 3N7, Canada
Stadium Olympic Stadium (capacity 61,000)
General Manager Position vacant at time of writing
Head Coach Jacques Dussault
Team Colours Maroon, silver and navy blue
1991 record 4–6 (3rd in North American East Division)

SCOUTING REPORT Now that inexperienced head coach Jacques Dussault has his rookie year behind him, Montreal Machine can reasonably expect to improve on their 1991 performance. They finished one game out of first place in their division without ever really being serious contenders for the title. However, if they are to take the next step forward they need to have improved their personnel in several key areas. Although their 27.8 third down conversion percentage, second worst in the league, and turnover ratio of minus twelve, which ranked dead last, may have been partly due to lack of coaching expertise, the Machine were let down largely by players failing to perform up to expectations.

This was particularly true at the quarterback position, where Kevin Sweeney, a former Dallas Cowboys starter, was Montreal's first-round selection and the second player chosen at that position in the entire draft. By Week Five he had lost the starting job to Michael Proctor. Sweeney threw just one touch-

● **Stan Gelbaugh of the Monarchs (10) finds a hole in the Montreal Machine defense.**

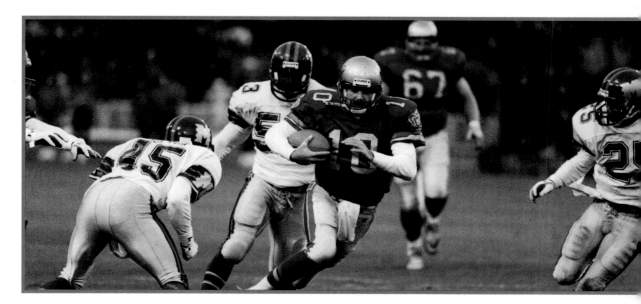

down pass in 69 attempts all season, completing less than 35 per cent of his passes for a horrible rating of 31.0. The subsequent performance of Proctor, however, suggests that Montreal should have gone into this season's draft with their sights set firmly on a new quarterback. Proctor, in his first professional job, threw only three scoring passes compared with 10 interceptions and connected on just 47.8 per cent of his passes. This left the Machine ranked last in passing offense with 115.8 yards per game.

On the ground, Montreal managed a second place ranking in yards gained, with an average gain of 4.1 placing them fifth among the league's rushing attacks. Once Elroy Harris had been waived midway through the season for an 'attitude problem', however, there was little spark left to ignite that area of the offense. Ricky Johnson's 3.8 yards per carry does not suggest he is capable of carrying the full load of the Montreal running game. The offensive line did little to help their team's cause, either. In the area of pass protection, the 44 sacks allowed by Montreal were topped only by the New York-New Jersey Knights' run-and-shoot formation.

Defensively, the Machine finished the season ranked eighth, although they proved reasonably effective at stopping the running game. Led by linebacker Tracy Simien, who returned to the NFL's Kansas City Chiefs – probably for good – after the season, they gave up only five rushing touchdowns, and opponents found that passing against Montreal was by far the easier option. Ranked ninth in defense against the pass, Montreal allowed only 47.8 per cent of attempts against them to be completed, but frequently gave up big plays. Each completion against them was worth 16.5 yards and they averaged less than one interception per game. Montreal also featured one of the weakest pass rushes in the league, recording just 22 sacks, which left opposing quarterbacks free to throw 20 touchdown passes. Apart from Simien, their one other imposing figure on the defense was All-World League second-team cornerback Richard Shelton, who also helped the Montreal return teams to feature among the most productive in the league. Shelton went the distance on a punt return and kick return in the same match against Sacramento, while little wide receiver Mike

Cadore was a constant threat on kick-offs. On the other side of the coin, Montreal allowed a league-high 21.6 yards on kick returns. The Machine boasted the best punter-kicker combination in the league, with Chris Mohr leading all punters with a 42.7 yard average and Bjorn Nittmo proving his accuracy from all distances, including four successes out of six from 40–49 yards.

HEAD COACH Jacques Dussault returned to Montreal, the city where he held his first professional coaching job as an assistant with the CFL's Montreal Alouettes from 1982 to 1985. In 1986 he was a coach at Michigan State, returning to the Alouettes in 1987 to serve as technical advisor and camp coordinator for the young Alouettes. He went to Paris in 1988 to act as head coach of the Anges Bleus and was guest coach at Boston University in the spring of 1989. Dussault spent the next two football seasons coaching and building a team at Mount Allison University in Sackville, New Brunswick.

RUSHING	No	Yds	Avg	Lng	TD
Johnson	110	423	3.8	20t	1
Harris, E.†	56	250	4.5	41t	2
Proctor	41	247	6.0	26	2
Sweeney†	19	84	4.4	24	0
Sargent	36	83	2.3	12	1
Harris, D.	17	71	4.2	25	1
Flynn	1	8	8.0	8	0
Cadore	2	–4	–2.0	–2	0
Mohr	3	–4	–1.3	4	0
TEAM	285	1158	4.1	41t	7

PUNT RETURNS	Ret	Fc	Yds	Avg	Lng	TD
Shelton	25	9	228	9.1	67t	1
Harris, W.†	3	0	13	4.3	10	0
Williams	1	0	6	6.0	6	0
TEAM	29	9	247	8.5	67t	1

INTERCEPTIONS	No	Yds	Avg	Lng	TD
Shelton	3	65	21.7	63t	1
Lofton	2	16	8.0	16	0
Jones, Q.	1	26	26.0	26	0
Jackson	1	12	12.0	12	0
Austin	1	9	9.0	9	0
Holmes	1	0	0.0	0	0
TEAM	9	128	14.2	63t	1

● Montreal running
back Ricky Johnson (34) is
grounded by London
Monarchs safety Harvey
Wilson (42).

KICK-OFF RETURNS	No	Yds	Avg	Lng	TD
Cadore	14	327	23.4	56	0
Harris, D.	22	338	15.4	28	0
Shelton	2	108	54.0	90t	1
Snead	2	82	41.0	63	0
Sargent	1	15	15.0	15	0
TEAM	**41**	**870**	**21.2**	**90t**	**2**

†Not on roster at end of season

RECEIVING	No	Yds	Avg	Lng	TD
Dunn	31	321	10.4	31	1
Sargent	23	209	9.1	35	0
Snead	16	212	13.3	51	1
Cooper	14	178	12.7	39	0
Johnson	13	157	12.1	22	0
Harris, D.	10	77	7.7	22	0
Cadore	7	89	12.7	24	0
Harris, E.†	7	25	3.6	22	0
Williams	4	81	20.3	53	0
Jennings†	4	54	13.5	21	1
Fumi	2	38	19.0	35	1
TEAM	**131**	**1441**	**11.0**	**53**	**4**

● **1991 RESULTS** ●

Mar 23	at Birmingham	W	20–5	(53,000)
Apr 1	Barcelona	L	10–34	(53,238)
Apr 8	Birmingham	W	23–10	(27,766)
Apr 13	New York-New Jersey	L	0–44	(34,821)
Apr 20	at London	L	7–45	(35,294)
Apr 27	at Frankfurt	L	7–17	(25,269)
May 4	at Sacramento	W	26–23	(17,326)
May 13	Raleigh-Durham	W	15–6	(20,123)
May 19	at San Antonio	L	10–27	(20,234)
May 27	Orlando	L	27–33	(23,493)

SACKS

Savage 6.5; Simien 4; Putzier 3; Carter 2; Murray 2;
Royal 2; Austin 1; Jones, T. 1; Gilbert 0.5. **TEAM: 22**

KICKING	FG1-19	20-29	30-39	40-49	50+	PAT	Pts
Nittmo	1/1	1/2	6/7	4/6	1/2	12/13	51

PUNTING	No	Yds	Avg	Net	TB	In20	Lng	Blk
Mohr	57	2436	42.7	34.0	5	13	58	2

● **1992 SCHEDULE** ●

Sun, Mar 22	at San Antonio
Sat, Mar 28	Orlando
Sat, Apr 4	at Sacramento
Sun, Apr 12	Ohio
Sun, Apr 19	at Orlando
Sun, Apr 26	New York-New Jersey
Sun, May 3	Sacramento
Sun, May 10	at Birmingham
Sun, May 17	London
Sat, May 23	at New York-New Jersey

PASSING	Att	Cmp	Yds	Cmp%	Yds/Att	TD	TD%	Int	Int%	Lng	Rating
Proctor	224	107	1222	47.8	5.46	3	1.3	10	4.5	53	50.5
Sweeney†	69	24	219	34.8	3.17	1	1.4	3	4.3	22	31.0
Mohr	1	0	0	0.0	0.00	0	0.0	1	100.0	0	0.0
Williams	1	0	0	0.0	0.00	0	0.0	0	0.0	0	0.0
TEAM	**285**	**131**	**1441**	**44.4**	**4.88**	**4**	**1.4**	**14**	**4.7**	**53**	**44.2**

●

MONTREAL MACHINE roster

No	Name	Pos	Ht	Wt	Born	College	How Acqd
22	Austin, Teryl	S	6-0	192	3/3/65	Pittsburgh	D12
94	Adam, Bob	LB	6-2	268	30/10/67	Texas A&M	D7
71	Brown, Tony	T	6-4	274	11/7/64	Pittsburgh	FA
81	Cadore, Mike	WR	5-8	169	11/6/68	Eastern Kentucky	D1
70	Carter, Johnny	NT	6-2	336	23/4/65	Grambling State	D9
30	Charles, Hency	CB	5-10	190	4/10/70	(Canada)	DIS
83	Cooper, Gary	WR	6-2	193	14/12/66	Clemson	BIR
8	Dacus, David	QB	6-0	211	25/5/66	Houston	ORL
73	DesRochers, Dave	T	6-6	296	1/12/64	San Diego State	D5
86	Dunn, K. D.	TE	6-4	213	28/4/63	Clemson	D2
1	Flynn, Chris	QB	6-1	190	17/11/66	(Canada)	DIS
80	Fumi, Steve	TE	6-4	240	24/2/67	Miami	LON
72	Gilbert, O'Neill	DE	6-2	267	29/3/65	Texas A&M	BAR
50	Graham, Dan	C	6-3	254	10/5/65	Northern Illinois	FA
31	Gray, Jamie	CB	6-0	205	13/2/69	(Canada)	DIS
21	Harris, Darryl	RB	5-10	193	20/2/66	Arizona State	D2
20	Holmes, Darryl	S	6-2	210	6/9/64	Ft Valley State	D5
36	Jackson, Orsorio	CB	6-0	194	15/9/68	Tennessee State	D2
34	Johnson, Ricky	RB	6-0	202	7/3/68	Maryland	D5
25	Jones, Quintin	CB	5-11	198	28/7/66	Pittsburgh	D1
26	Jones, Tyrone	S	6-3	241	9/11/66	Arkansas State	D6
10	Kasowski, Steve	K	6-1	189	18/7/66	(Canada)	DIS
62	Kelley, Mike	G	6-4	265	27/2/62	Notre Dame	FA
64	Kula, Bob	G	6-3	281	24/8/67	Michigan	D2
67	Lightner, Kevin	G	6-1	288	4/7/66	Nebraska	D3
92	Little, George	T	6-3	275	27/6/63	Iowa	FA
45	Lofton, Steve	CB	5-9	180	26/11/68	Texas A&M	D3
11	Mohr, Chris	P	6-5	218	11/5/66	Alabama	D1
57	Murray, Dan	LB	6-1	237	20/10/66	East Stroudsburg	D2
3	Nittmo, Bjorn	K	5-11	182	26/7/66	Appalachian State	D1
79	Novak, Jeff	T	6-5	277	27/7/67	South-West Texas	D1
14	Proctor, Michael	QB	6-4	204	14/7/67	Murray State	D4
76	Putzier, Rollin	DL	6-4	303	10/12/65	Oregon	D3
90	Royal, Desmond	NT	6-0	292	16/11/66	Texas Tech	D5
47	Sargent, Broderick	RB	5-10	229	16/9/62	Baylor	D2
55	Savage, Ray	LB	6-1	245	3/1/68	Virginia	D1
42	Shelton, Richard	CB	5-9	200	2/1/66	Liberty	D2
53	Simien, Tracy	LB	6-1	245	21/5/67	Texas Christian	NFL
84	Snead, Willie	WR	5-11	193	3/9/66	Florida	D2
59	Walls, Henry	LB	6-1	230	13/2/64	Clemson	S4
82	Williams, Steve	WR	5-9	173	14/2/67	Illinois	SAC

Roster correct at end of 1991 season. Key to How Acquired column: D1 – first round draft pick; S4 – fourth round pick in supplementary draft; DIS – Operation Discovery; NFL – NFL enhancement allocation; FA – free agent; BIR – formerly with Birmingham; ORL – formerly with Orlando; LON – formerly with London; BAR – formerly with Barcelona; SAC – formerly with Sacramento

NEW YORK-NEW JERSEY KNIGHTS

Address 150 East 58th Street, 22nd Floor, New York, NY 10155
Stadium Giants Stadium (capacity 75,000)
General Manager Reggie Williams
Head Coach Darrel 'Mouse' Davis
Team Colours Black, silver and gold
1991 record 5–5 (North American East Division champions), beaten in semi-final play-offs

SCOUTING REPORT The New York-New Jersey Knights will need to find a way to beat the World League's better teams if they are to make a serious challenge in 1992. Including their semi-final loss to London, the Knights went 0–6 in 1991 against teams who either made the play-offs or posted a winning record. They got fat against the weaker opposition, achieving a 5–0 record against non-play-off, non-winning teams, and scoring 194 of their season's total of 257 points in those games. The Knights – led by the bullying, Napoleonic figure of Darrel 'Mouse' Davis – deserve some credit, however, for rebounding from an 0–3 start to win their division when they could easily have written the season off after the first three weeks.

Davis's boast that the 'run-and-shoot cannot be stopped' will continue to be a source of embarrassment to him this season unless he has been able to find some help on the offensive line. The unfortunate New York quarterbacks, in particular Jeff Graham, were sacked a staggering 68 times last season. As well as costing the Knights 47.6 yards per game, it could easily have cost them Graham's services had he not proved so resilient in the face of such punishment. Graham and the Knights may not be so fortunate this time. At least Davis had the satisfaction of seeing the Knights finish second in offensive yardage, including

second in passing. Graham performed heroically to finish with a quarterback rating of 84.6, third best in the league, and although the temptation must have been there to simply throw the ball anywhere to avoid some of the beating he absorbed, he was intercepted only eight times all season, less than three times for every 100 passes. Graham was surrounded in 1991 by the quartet of Lonnie Turner, Monty Gilbreath, Kip Lewis and Cornell Burbage, who proved their big-play potential by averaging more than 16 yards per catch between them. They were supplemented by running back Eric Wilkerson, who held four touchdown passes to add to his seven rushing touchdowns during the regular season.

It was Wilkerson who put the run into the run-and-shoot. Swift and graceful, he averaged an impressive 6.1 yards on just 117 carries to finish as the league's rushing leader with 717 yards. Admittedly, his success was helped by opponents keying on the pass, but it will be interesting to see what happens this season if the Knights choose to find a way of putting the ball into Wilkerson's hands more often. The traditional problems of the run-and-shoot in scoring from close to the opponents' end zone were solved largely by Graham, who got the job done himself with six rushing touchdowns.

While most attention was focussed on the Knights' offense, the defense put together a solid season, finishing as the third-ranked unit and helping the Knights to a healthy takeaway/giveaway ratio of plus eleven. Using a four-man front, they limited opponents to four rushing touchdowns, while ends Tony Woods and Craig Schlichting combined for 14 sacks out of a team total of 43, second best in the league. The stars of the Knights defense, however, lived in the secondary, where cornerback Anthony Parker and safety Falanda Newton, one of the year's most unlikely successes, fed off errant passes like vultures. Parker, the league's co-Defensive MVP, finished with eleven interceptions, while Newton, a last-round selection in the draft pick, helped himself to eight as the Knights led the league with 21. The Knights defense proved adept at preventing opponents making important plays, with only 25.9 per cent of third down attempts against them ending in success.

New York's special teams left much to be desired and require improvement in virtually every area. Their return teams were unproductive, while the coverage units were among the most generous. The Knights desperately need a reliable kicker after seeing Barry Belli and Kendall Trainor make only three out of nine field goal attempts from 30 yards-plus. Only the performance of punter Bob Lilljedahl, averaging 42.3 yards, was a source of encouragement.

HEAD COACH Darrel 'Mouse' Davis has become known as the father of the run-and-shoot, an explosive style of offense he first introduced to the American public in his role as offensive coordinator of the USFL's Houston Gamblers in 1984. With Jim Kelly, now of the Buffalo Bills, at quarterback, the Gamblers averaged 427 yards and 34.3 points per game. Davis was appointed head coach of the Denver Gold in 1985 and led them to an 11–7 record in the USFL. After serving as director of football operations for the Arena League in 1987, he joined the NFL's Detroit Lions as offensive assistant in 1988. Davis became offensive coordinator for the 1989 and 1990 seasons and installed the Lions' 'Silver Stretch' offense. Davis's first head coaching job was at Portland State University from 1975 to 1980, the team finishing first in the nation in passing and total offense every season. He entered the professional ranks as offensive coordinator of the Canadian Football League's Toronto Argonauts.

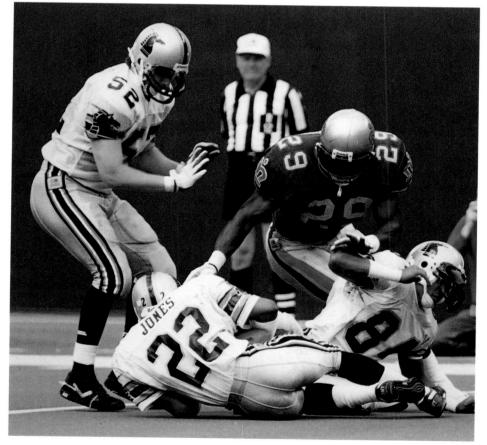

Knights trio Ron Sancho (52), Tony Jones (22) and Monty Gilbreath (81) take on the Monarchs.

THE WORLD LEAGUE OF AMERICAN FOOTBALL 1992

PASSING	Att	Cmp	Yds	Cmp%	Yds/Att	TD	TD%	Int	Int%	Lng	Rating
Graham	272	157	2407	57.7	8.85	8	2.9	8	2.9	64t	84.6
Hammel	55	25	321	45.5	5.84	2	3.6	3	5.5	39	53.7
Newton	2	0	0	0.0	0.00	0	0.0	0	0.0	0	39.6
Trainor*	1	0	0	0.0	0.00	0	0.0	0	100.0	0	0.0
TEAM	329	182	2728	55.3	8.29	10	3.0	11	3.3	64t	78.9

RUSHING	No	Yds	Avg	Lng	TD
Wilkerson	117	717	6.1	74	7
Graham	46	140	3.0	24	6
Jeffery	16	72	4.5	22	2
Hammel	13	58	4.5	17	1
Yuma	6	23	3.8	11	0
Newton	1	0	0.0	0	0
TEAM	199	1010	5.1	74	16

PUNT RETURNS	Ret	Fc	Yds	Avg	Lng	TD
Alexander	20	2	143	7.2	29	0
Burbage	11	6	48	4.4	14	0
Turner	1	0	0	0.0	0	0
TEAM	32	8	191	6.0	18	0

KICK-OFF RETURNS	No	Yds	Avg	Lng	TD
Hardy	11	213	19.4	29	0
Burbage	8	136	17.0	22	0
Jones	6	141	23.5	49	0
Courville	3	24	8.0	15	0
Collins	1	9	9.0	9	0
Sancho	1	0	0.0	0	0
TEAM	30	523	17.4	49	0

RECEIVING	No	Yds	Avg	Lng	TD
Turner	41	629	15.3	52	1
Gilbreath	40	643	16.1	46	1
Lewis	29	475	16.4	64t	2
Wilkerson	26	273	10.5	25t	4
Burbage	22	419	19.0	49	1
Lockett	9	97	10.8	26	1
Hardy	7	69	9.9	15	0
Alexander	4	63	15.8	39	0
Jeffery	4	60	15.0	20	0
TEAM	182	2728	15.0	64t	10

*Stats for Sacramento and New York-New Jersey
†Not on roster at end of season

INTERCEPTIONS	No	Yds	Avg	Lng	TD
Parker	11	270	24.5	46t	2
Newton	8	104	13.0	46	0
Jones	2	0	0.0	0	0
Moore	0	16	—	16	0
TEAM	21	390	18.6	46t	2

● 1991 RESULTS ●

Mar 24	at Barcelona	L	7–19	(19,223)
Mar 31	at London	L	18–22	(46,952)
Apr 6	Frankfurt	L	17–27	(36,546)
Apr 13	at Montreal	W	44–0	(34,821)
Apr 22	Sacramento	W	28–20	(21,230)
Apr 27	Orlando	W	42–6	(30,046)
May 5	at Raleigh-Durham	W	42–6	(10,069)
May 11	London	L	7–22	(41,219)
May 20	at Birmingham	L	14–24	(31,500)
May 25	San Antonio	W	38–9	(32,857)

SACKS

Campbell 7.5; Woods 7.5; Schlichting 6.5; Sancho 6; Marlatt 4; Courville 3; Edeen 3; Newton 1.5; Jones 1; Mikolas 1; Moore 1; Fletcher 0.5; Jackson 0.5. TEAM: 43

KICKING	FG1-19	20-29	30-39	40-49	50+	PAT	Pts
Trainor*	0/0	4/4	2/5	3/7	0/0	12/14	39
Belli†	0/0	3/4	1/2	1/4	0/2	25/25	40
TEAM	0/0	3/4	1/3	2/6	0/2	33/33	51

● 1992 SCHEDULE ●

Sun, Mar 22	at London
Sat, Mar 28	at Barcelona
Sat, Apr 4	San Antonio
Sun, Apr 12	at Orlando
Sat, Apr 18	Frankfurt
Sun, Apr 26	at Montreal
Sun, May 3	London
Sun, May 10	at Ohio
Sat, May 16	Barcelona
Sat, May 23	Montreal

PUNTING	No	Yds	Avg	Net	TB	In20	Lng	Blk
Lilljedahl	39	1651	42.3	33.1	4	9	62	1
Trainor*	29	946	32.6	31.7	1	3	56	0
Belli†	10	312	31.2	25.6	1	0	41	1
TEAM	51	1963	38.5	31.5	5	9	62	2

NEW YORK-NEW JERSEY KNIGHTS roster

No	Name	Pos	Ht	Wt	Born	College	How Acqd
80	Alexander, Andre	WR	5-5	168	15/4/67	Fresno State	FA
72	Beun, Daniel	OL	6-4	255	15/4/62	(Belgium)	DIS
82	Burbage, Cornell	WR	5-10	189	22/2/65	Kentucky	D1
99	Campbell, Joe	LB	6-4	249	28/12/66	New Mexico State	D1
56	Collins, Fabray	LB	6-2	220	16/9/61	Southern Illinois	FA
21	Courville, Vince	CB	5-10	160	5/12/59	Rice	S4
93	Edeen, David	DE	6-3	260	23/5/66	Wyoming	D3
10	Evans, John	QB	6-5	200	6/9/67	Lamar University	EA
58	Fletcher, Cecil	LB	6-1	228	12/7/65	Marshall	D7
81	Gilbreath, Monty	WR	5-7	190	24/10/68	San Diego State	D4
9	Graham, Jeff	QB	6-4	211	5/2/66	Long Beach State	S2
53	Haering, Chris	LB	6-1	224	10/6/67	West Virginia	D3
5	Hammel, Todd	QB	6-1	211	7/12/66	Stephen F. Austin	D1
84	Hardy, Anthony	WR	5-8	151	13/4/66	Purdue	FA
54	Holder, Rod	C	6-1	283	30/4/67	Miami	FA
26	Howard, James	CB	5-11	177	5/4/66	Fullerton State	D10
74	Husar, Mike	G	6-2	302	27/6/66	Michigan	D5
77	Jackson, Les	DE	6-5	287	23/8/63	(England)	DIS
27	Jeffery, Tony	RB	5-11	215	9/7/64	Texas Christian	FA
22	Jones, Tony	CB	5-10	183	4/1/67	Florida	D2
88	Lewis, Kip	WR	5-9	166	6/2/67	Arizona	D2
4	Lilljedahl, Bob	P	6-4	229	9/12/66	Texas	FA
83	Lockett, Charles	WR	5-10	190	1/10/65	Long Beach State	FRA
94	Marlatt, Pat	DT	6-5	260	3/5/66	West Virginia	D4
69	Mikolas, Doug	DE	6-1	260	7/6/61	Portland State	S6
25	Moore, Mark	S	5-11	204	3/9/64	Oklahoma	D7
49	Newton, Falanda	S	6-1	198	18/4/67	Texas Christian	D12
31	Parker, Anthony	CB	5-9	166	6/2/67	Arizona	D2
71	Rentie, Caesar	T	6-2	290	10/11/64	Oklahoma	D1
52	Sancho, Ron	LB	6-2	228	21/6/65	Louisiana State	D2
91	Schlichting, Craig	DE	6-5	273	14/3/66	Wyoming	D2
51	Scott, Pete	C	6-4	285	6/10/68	Missouri	D8
60	Searels, Stacy	T	6-5	285	19/5/65	Auburn	D2
64	Simons, Kevin	T	6-3	311	25/4/67	Tennessee	FA
28	Taylor, Michael	S	6-0	171	2/3/64	(England)	DIS
7	Trainor, Kendall	K	6-1	222	8/7/67	Arkansas	SAC
86	Turner, Lonnie	WR	5-7	168	31/8/60	Cal Poly-Pomona	S5
76	Warne, Jim	T	6-6	311	27/11/64	Arizona State	D10
40	Wilkerson, Eric	RB	5-9	181	19/12/66	Kent State	D1
91	Woods, Tony	DE	6-3	272	16/3/66	Oklahoma	D1
41	Yuma, Eric	RB	6-0	194	5/5/69	(Belgium)	DIS

Roster correct at end of 1991 season. Key to How Acquired column: D1 – first round draft pick; S2 – second round pick in supplementary draft; FA – free agent; DIS – Operation Discovery; FRA – formerly with Frankfurt; SAC – formerly with Sacramento; EA – extra allocation draft

ORLANDO THUNDER

Address 800 North Magnolia Avenue, Suite 700, Orlando, Florida 32803
Stadium Florida Citrus Bowl (capacity 70,000)
General Manager Dick Beam
Head Coach Galen Hall
Team Colours Lime green, light blue and royal blue
1991 record 5–5 (2nd in North American East Division)

SCOUTING REPORT Galen Hall, offensive co-ordinator last season, will have to turn his attention to improving the league's worst defense if the Thunder are to mark his first season as head coach by winning the North American East Division. Only the hapless Raleigh-Durham Skyhawks gave up more than the 286 points allowed by Orlando in 1991 and even in the five games the team won they conceded an average of 25.6 points. After beginning the season with two spectacular high scoring victories, Orlando's weaknesses were exposed in the tougher part of their schedule and their successes all came against clubs who ended the season with losing records.

Offensively, it was feast or famine for the Thunder, who averaged 38.2 points in the games they won, but failed to top 14 points in any of their defeats. Their flamboyant style of offense may have fooled the league's weaker teams, but the play-off chasing sides had Orlando's number, leaving them ranked seventh in offensive yards. On the ground, Orlando were the seventh-ranked club, but only the run-and-shoot New York-New Jersey Knights had less use for their rushers than the Thunder. When they did run the ball, their 4.4 average gain was third best in the league, and the versatile Eric Mitchel (6.7 average on 42 attempts) proved just the man to exploit opposition surprise. After beginning the season with nine touch-

down passes in two games, quarterback Kerwin Bell averaged only one per game for the rest of the year, throwing a further 13 interceptions in the same period. His final rating of 76.4, fourth best in the league, was solid enough, as was his 55.2 completion percentage, but the Orlando fans had expected more after the former University of Florida star's magnificent overture. Receiver Byron Williams was sensational all season long, a combination of grace, speed and durability which saw him finish second in the league in receptions (59) and yards (811) and tying for the league lead with 11 touchdowns.

There were no such success stories on the other side of the ball, however. The Thunder defense ranked eighth against the run, and dead last versus the pass. No defense in the league was more accommodating for offenses facing third down situations, 39.6 per cent of which were converted into first downs. Orlando managed to apply occasional pressure on opposing quarterbacks from most areas, including seven sacks from the safety positions, but they were one of the easier teams to complete passes against (53.2 per cent). In addition, they posed little threat in the interception department: their meagre eight pick-offs was the lowest total of any team.

One area in which Orlando could claim to be number one with little fear of contradiction was their return teams. Carl Painter was the league's most consistent kick-off returner, averaging almost 25 yards on 24 attempts without the help of any return above 48 yards. The end-to-end stuff was left to his deputies, Mitchel and Erroll Tucker, who each went 90 yards-plus for a touchdown. Tucker was electrifying on the punt team as well, leading the league with a 20.7 average, including a 66-yard

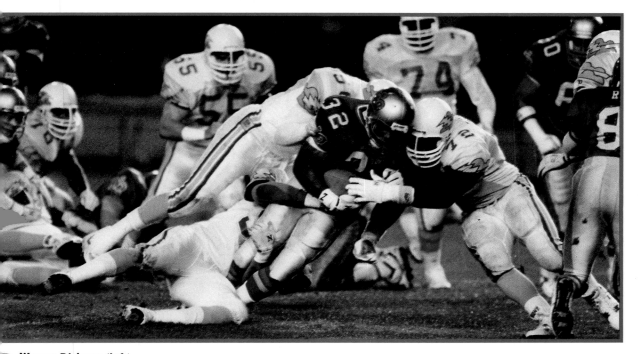

**Wayne Dickson (left)
and Robert Prestbury (right).**

ouchdown. Orlando's other special team units were modest, with kicker Charlie Baumann struggling from ong range and finding the target with only two of even attempts of 40 yards or longer.

EAD COACH Galen Hall is one of the most amous footballing names in the state of Florida ollowing an illustrious 27-year coaching career. His reatest success came during a five-year reign as ead coach at the University of Florida, where he ook charge in 1984 with the Gators struggling at —1—1. Hall's team reeled off eight successive ictories to finish the season ranked number one in he nation by the Sporting News and earn Hall Coach f the Year honours from the Associated Press. His uiet, calm approach to the game led Florida to top ve finishes in the AP poll in 1984 and 1985, during hich time his 17—1—1 coaching record was second est in the nation.

Hall's coaching career began at the University of Vest Virginia in 1964 and continued at Oklahoma in 966, the beginning of an 18-year spell with the ooners, for whom he was offensive coordinator for n years. During his time at Oklahoma, the team on two national championships, 10 Big Eight

Conference titles and appeared in 13 bowl games, as well as regularly being ranked among the top three teams in the country in the categories of rushing offense, total offense and scoring.

● 1991 RESULTS ●					
Mar 25	San Antonio	W	35–34	(21,714)
Mar 30	Raleigh-Durham	W	58–20	(20,811)
Apr 6	at London	L	12–35	(35,327)
Apr 14	at Barcelona	L	13–33	(40,875)
Apr 21	Birmingham	L	6–31	(21,249)
Apr 27	at New York-New Jersey	L	6–42	(30,046)
May 4	Frankfurt	L	14–17	(11,270)
May 11	Sacramento	W	45–33	(20,048)
May 20	at Raleigh-Durham	W	20–14	(4,207)
May 27	at Montreal	W	33–27	(23,493)

● 1992 SCHEDULE ●	
Sun, Mar	Ohio
Sat, Mar 28	at Montreal
Sun, Apr 5	at Ohio
Sun, Apr 12	New York-New Jersey
Sun, Apr 19	Montreal
Sat, Apr 25	at Frankfurt
Sun, May 3	at San Antonio
Sat, May 9	London
Sun, May 17	at Birmingham
Sat, May 23	Barcelona

PASSING	Att	Cmp	Yds	Cmp%	Yds/Att	TD	TD%	Int	Int%	Lng	Rating
Bell	325	181	2214	55.7	6.81	17	5.2	14	4.3	75t	76.4
Peterson	20	9	99	45.0	4.95	1	5.0	0	0.0	21	76.9
Mitchel	1	1	53	100.0	53.0	1	100.0	0	0.0	53t	158.3
TEAM	346	191	2366	55.2	6.85	19	5.5	14	4.0	75t	78.0

RUSHING	No	Yds	Avg	Lng	TD
Jones, M.	68	288	4.2	20	2
Mitchel	42	281	6.7	58	3
Stowers	38	167	4.4	17	1
Bell	25	55	2.2	12	0
Painter	15	47	3.1	18	0
Peterson	9	45	5.0	18	0
Williams, B.	6	18	3.0	17	0
TEAM	203	901	4.4	58	6

RECEIVING	No	Yds	Avg	Lng	TD
Williams, B.	59	811	13.7	42t	11
Mitchel	26	213	12.0	75t	1
LaSane	23	333	14.5	53t	3
Roscoe	20	225	11.3	39t	2
Simpson	18	239	13.3	39	2
Stowers	18	156	18.7	23	0
Jones, M.	14	133	19.5	17	0
Painter	13	157	12.1	26	0
TEAM	191	2366	12.4	75t	19

KICK-OFF RETURNS	No	Yds	Avg	Lng	TD
Painter	24	597	24.9	48	0
Mitchel	8	276	34.5	96t	1
Tucker	7	259	37.0	95t	1
Flannigan†	3	49	16.3	18	0
Jackson, Chris	3	49	16.3	18	0
Jones, D.*	2	21	10.5	11	0
Jones, M.	1	8	8.0	8	0
LaSane	1	0	0.0	0	0
Nettles	1	18	18.0	18	0
TEAM	48	1256	26.2	96t	2

*Stats for Sacramento and Orlando
†Not on roster at end of season

INTERCEPTIONS	No	Yds	Avg	Lng	TD
Nettles	3	48	16.0	34	0
Tucker	2	1	0.5	1	0
Walker	2	−4	−2.0	0	0
Owens	1	0	0.0	0	0
Sterling†	0	33	—	33t	1
TEAM	8	78	9.8	34	1

PUNT RETURNS	Ret	Fc	Yds	Avg	Lng	TD
Tucker	18	10	373	20.7	66t	1

SACKS

Bryant 7; Dickson 5; Jackson, Cha. 4; Owens 4; Walker 4; Nettles 3; Covington 2; Davis, R. 1; Davis, W. 1; Massey 1; Williams, C.† 1. **TEAM: 33**

KICKING	FG1-19	20-29	30-39	40-49	50+	PAT	Pts
Baumann	1/1	3/3	4/5	2/7	0/0	24/26	54

PUNTING	No	Yds	Avg	Net	TB	In20	Lng	Blk
Criswell	46	1827	39.7	33.5	4	10	56	0

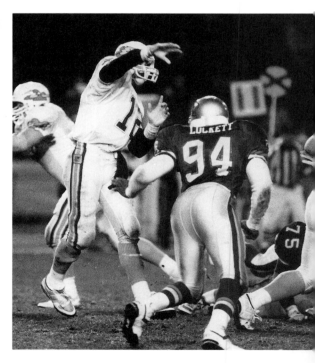

Kerwin Bell (12) fade after a fast start.

ORLANDO THUNDER roster

No	Name	Pos	Ht	Wt	Born	College	How Acqd
65	Aronson, Doug	G	6-2	274	14/8/64	San Diego State	D3
6	Baumann, Charlie	K	6-1	203	25/8/67	West Virginia	D7
12	Bell, Kerwin	QB	6-2	199	15/6/65	Florida	D1
92	Brown, Henry	DE	6-2	242	27/1/65	Florida	S4
70	Bryant, Winfred	DE	6-3	280	7/11/66	Nicholls State	D1
26	Covington, Brian	CB	6-0	165	23/10/68	Central Florida	D8
2	Criswell, Ray	P	6-0	191	16/8/63	Florida	D1
71	Davis, Richard	NT	6-0	256		Arizona State	SAC
57	Davis, Wayne	LB	6-2	218	10/3/64	Alabama	D1
56	Dickson, Wayne	LB	6-2	248	27/11/67	Oklahoma	D3
73	Durden, John	T	6-6	295	2/8/67	Florida	D7
75	Foust, Mike	T	6-4	278	13/11/66	Fresno State	D10
38	Franklin, Harvey	CB	5-11	182	7/6/67	(Netherlands)	DIS
61	Guerrero, John	G	6-3	325	13/12/65	Southern California	D2
64	Hooven, Owen	T	6-8	331	11/8/66	Oregon State	D8
74	Jackson, Charles	NT	6-3	288	4/8/66	Jackson State	D9
22	Jackson, Chris	RB	5-8	179	25/9/64	Boise State	S6
94	Joder, Helmut	DE	6-5	225	22/10/66	(Germany)	DIS
44	Jones, DeWaine	RB	5-10	203	14/12/67	Wyoming	SAC
25	Jones, Myron	RB	5-9	197	24/2/68	Fresno State	D1
87	LaSane, Bruce	WR	6-3	209	24/3/67	Florida State	D7
52	Lossow, Rodney	C	6-2	272	28/8/65	Wisconsin	D4
55	Massey, Tony	LB	6-2	221	4/11/65	Kentucky	BAR
51	Massimiani, John	LB	6-1	227	3/8/67	Kent State	D8
21	Mitchel, Eric	RB	5-11	197	13/2/67	Oklahoma	D2
82	Nagurski, Steffen	TE	6-3	235	7/11/69	(Germany)	DIS
23	Nettles, Mike	S	5-10	194	24/8/67	Memphis State	D6
42	Owens, Billy	S	6-1	199	2/12/65	Pittsburgh	D4
27	Painter, Carl	RB	5-10	180	10/5/64	Hampton	S7
5	Peterson, Tim	QB	6-3	214	28/12/67	Wisconsin	D3
72	Presbury, Robert	DE	6-2	251	18/7/65	Delaware State	D4
53	Reesing, Dirk	LB	6-2	245	19/4/66	(Germany)	DIS
89	Roscoe, Chris	WR	6-1	211	6/7/68	Hawaii	D5
83	Simpson, John	WR	5-11	167	24/2/66	Baylor	D2
30	Smith, Richard	CB	5-11	194	29/10/66	Clemson	R-D
37	Stowers, Tommie	RB	6-3	234	18/11/66	Missouri	D1
20	Tucker, Erroll	CB	5-7	167	6/7/64	Utah	D1
95	Walker, Willie	LB	6-1	243	8/4/67	North Carolina	S5
88	Williams, Byron	WR	6-1	178	31/10/60	Texas-Arlington	S3
28	Williams, Steve	CB	6-0	197	18/12/66	Boston College	BAR
77	Withycombe, Mike	T	6-5	312	18/11/64	Fresno State	D1

Roster correct at end of 1991 season. Key to How Acquired column: D1 – first round draft pick; S3 – third round pick in supplementary draft; DIS – Operation Discovery; SAC – formerly with Sacramento; BAR – formerly with Barcelona; R-D – formerly with Raleigh-Durham

SACRAMENTO SURGE

Address 14670 Cantova Way, Rancho Murieta, CA 95683
Stadium To be announced (1991: Hughes Stadium, capacity 23,000)
General Manager Michael F. Keller
Head Coach Kay Stephenson
Team Colours Aqua and light gold
1991 record 3–7 (3rd in North American West Division)

SCOUTING REPORT An improvement on the defensive side of the ball should be the number one priority for head coach Kay Stephenson as he leads Sacramento into action on the back of a disappointing 1991 season. If it had not been for their inexplicable dominance of Frankfurt – whom they beat twice – the Surge would have had only their 9–3 opening game victory over the Raleigh-Durham Skyhawks to show for their efforts, a state of affairs due largely to their failure to stop opposition offenses.

Their own offense performed encouragingly after a slow start, scoring at least 20 points in each of Sacramento's final six games – but that was good enough for only one victory. The fifth highest scoring team in the league, the Surge ranked sixth in yardage, but could have used a dominant figure in the backfield. Victor Floyd and first-round draft pick Paul Frazier shared the load of the rushing game and were solid, without ever causing opponents to lose too much sleep.

The passing game was entrusted to the arm of Mike Elkins, who joined the Surge from the roster of the Kansas City Chiefs as part of the NFL's enhancement programme. The former Wake Forest signal-caller failed to enhance the Sacramento offense as much as they had hoped. Although recording three 300-yard games, Elkins was inconsistent, throwing for as many interceptions as touchdowns and completing less than half his passes. The Chiefs saw enough to decide he lacked the tools of an NFL quarterback and cut him before the 1991 season, but he could yet develop into an efficient World League player. When Elkins was on song, he had top-class accompaniment from wide receiver Carl Parker, whose 52 catches and 801 yards both ranked third in the league. Sacramento would like to feature a receiver of similar ability this year to prevent teams double-teaming Parker, the only Surge wide-out to catch more than 20 passes. The offense did itself few favours by converting only 26 per cent of their third downs, the worst success rate in the league. Maybe it would have been different if they had faced their own defense, who allowed 35.3 per cent of third downs to be converted, generosity which only two other teams could match.

Sacramento were also a soft touch against the run, despite the presence of All-World League second-teamer Pete Najarian at inside linebacker. They ranked ninth in yards allowed, although the 4.6 yards they gave up at a time made them the easiest team to move the ball against, and no club yielded more rushing touchdowns than the Surge total of sixteen. Sacramento's pass defense was far healthier, with safety Greg Coauette thriving sufficiently to become the Surge's only presence on the All-World League first team. Not only did the former USC star grab three interceptions, but he also provided much of the Sacramento pass rush, tying for the team lead with four sacks. Opposing quarterbacks were restricted to completing only 47.3 per cent of their passes, and threw just one touchdown pass every alternate game. Fourteen interceptions left the Surge ranked fourth in the league to go with fifth place in yardage allowed.

The Surge special teams were poor. Despite using a whole committee of kick-off returners, they failed ever to advance further than 33 yards, finishing the year with an 18.2 yard average, one of the league's lowest. Their performances on punt returns and opposition kick returns were equally discouraging. John Nies and Kendall Trainor, who ended the season with New York-New Jersey, proved a less than brilliant punting combination, while the same men combined to succeed on only 12 of 20 field goal attempts. Improvement is clearly needed in this area.

HEAD COACH Kay Stephenson entered the World League as one of its most experienced coaches. In contrast, he was the NFL's youngest coach when Chuck Knox appointed Stephenson to the Los Angeles Ram staff in 1977. As Rams quarterback coach, Stephenson worked with the legendary Joe Namath, but when Knox became head coach of the Buffalo Bills the following year he packed his bags and followed him East. As an offensive assistant, Stephenson helped the Bills reach the NFL play-offs in 1980 and 1981. At the end of the 1982 season Knox took the Seattle Seahawks job, but this time Stephenson stayed behind to take over as Buffalo head coach. He held the position until four games into the 1985 season, when he was fired after compiling a 10–26 record during his reign. A graduate of the University of Florida, Stephenson's injury-hit professional career included spells as quarterback at the San Diego Chargers and Buffalo Bills. His first pro coaching job was with the World Football League's Jacksonville Sharks, for whom he was offensive coordinator in 1974.

● **Surge running back Tony Burse (28).**

PASSING	Att	Cmp	Yds	Cmp%	Yds/Att	TD	TD%	Int	Int%	Lng	Rating
Elkins	312	153	2068	49.0	6.63	13	4.2	13	4.2	60t	67.1
Bennett†	26	9	60	34.6	2.31	2	7.7	10	7.7	10	11.4
Ellis	10	5	56	50.0	5.60	1	10.0	0	0.0	26	100.4
Frazier	1	0	0	0.0	0.00	0	0.0	0	0.0	0	39.6
Parker	1	0	0	0.0	0.00	0	0.0	0	0.0	0	39.6
Trainor†	1	0	0	0.0	0.00	0	0.0	1	100.0	0	0.0
TEAM	351	167	2184	47.6	6.22	14	4.0	16	4.6	60t	62.0

RUSHING	No	Yds	Avg	Lng	TD
Floyd	92	406	4.4	25	2
Frazier	90	308	3.4	31	3
Perry	28	160	5.7	26	1
Elkins	20	71	3.6	14	0
Burse	19	51	2.7	14	0
Farr	1	10	10.0	10	0
Bennett†	1	0	0.0	0	0
TEAM	251	1006	4.0	31	6

RECEIVING	No	Yds	Avg	Lng	TD
Parker	52	801	15.4	41	8
Farr	23	309	13.4	32t	1
Holloway	18	293	16.3	38	2
Frazier	15	106	7.1	29	0
Floyd	13	186	14.3	60t	1
Perry	13	95	7.3	16	0
Burse	13	72	5.5	16	0
Craig†	12	205	17.1	35	0
Archer†	4	43	10.8	20t	1
Sumner	2	52	26.0	41t	1
Cartwright	2	22	11.0	11	0
TEAM	167	2184	13.1	60t	14

KICK-OFF RETURNS	No	Yds	Avg	Lng	TD
Floyd	9	189	21.0	33	0
Frazier	7	123	17.6	28	0
Gaiters	5	101	20.2	25	0
Holloway	5	89	17.8	24	0
McWright	4	76	19.0	29	0
Searcy†	4	93	23.3	30	0
Craig†	3	61	20.3	23	0
Farr	2	24	12.0	12	0
Jones†	2	21	10.5	11	0
Kalombo†	1	0	0.0	0	0
Thompson	1	4	4.0	4	0
TEAM	43	781	18.2	33	0

†Not on roster at end of season

INTERCEPTIONS	No	Yds	Avg	Lng	TD
Adams	4	17	4.3	15	0
Coauette	3	24	8.0	11	0
Gerhart	2	8	4.0	8	0
Moore	1	12	12.0	12	0
Hall	1	7	7.0	7	0
Soltis	1	7	7.0	7	0
Malone	1	0	0.0	0	0
McWright	1	0	0.0	0	0
TEAM	14	75	5.4	15	0

PUNT RETURNS	Ret	Fc	Yds	Avg	Lng	TD
Parker	15	2	127	8.5	19	0
Searcy†	6	2	16	2.7	5	0
Gaiters	4	0	26	6.5	10	0
TEAM	25	4	169	6.8	19	0

SACKS

Coauette 4; Henton 4; Hill 4; Moore 4; Dominic 3; Sapolu 2; Knight 1.5; Gerhart 1; Soltis 1; Thompson 1; Zumwalt 1; Wallace 0.5. **TEAM: 28**

KICKING	FG1-19	20-29	30-39	40-49	50+	PAT	Pts
Trainor†	0/0	4/4	2/4	2/5	0/0	4/6	28
Nies	0/0	1/2	2/2	1/3	0/0	11/12	23
TEAM	0/0	5/6	4/6	3/8	0/0	15/18	51

PUNTING	No	Yds	Avg	Net	TB	In20	Lng	Blk
Nies	23	902	39.2	28.5	4	4	53	2
Trainor†	29	946	32.6	31.7	1	3	56	0
TEAM	54	1848	34.2	30.2	5	7	56	2

● 1991 RESULTS ●

Mar 23	Raleigh-Durham	W	9–3	(15,126)
Mar 30	at Birmingham	L	10–17	(16,500)
Apr 7	at San Antonio	L	3–10	(6,772)
Apr 13	Frankfurt	W	16–10	(17,065)
Apr 22	at New York–New Jersey	L	20–28	(21,230)
Apr 27	Barcelona	L	20–29	(19,045)
May 4	Montreal	L	23–26	(17,326)
May 11	at Orlando	L	33–45	(20,048)
May 18	London	L	21–45	(21,409)
May 25	at Frankfurt	W	24–13	(51,653)

● 1992 SCHEDULE ●

Sat, Mar 21	Birmingham
Sun, Mar 29	at Ohio
Sat, Apr 4	Montreal
Sat, Apr 11	San Antonio
Sat, Apr 18	at Birmingham
Sun, Apr 26	at London
Sun, May 3	at Montreal
Sat, May 9	Frankfurt
Sat, May 16	Ohio
Sat, May 23	at San Antonio

SACRAMENTO SURGE roster

No	Name	Pos	Ht	Wt	Born	College	How Acqd
27	Adams, Mike	CB	5-10	206	5/4/64	Arkansas State	D2
72	Buddenberg, John	G	6-4	279	9/10/66	Akron	D4
67	Burman, John	T	6-8	291	17/6/66	Illinois	D6
28	Burse, Tony	RB	6-0	217	4/4/64	Middle Tennessee	D4
83	Cartwright, Ricardo	CB	5-10	180	2/2/65	Florida A&M	D3
33	Coauette, Greg	S	6-2	207	29/10/64	Southern California	D5
65	Dominic, John	NT	6-2	271	20/7/65	Syracuse	D4
10	Elkins, Mike	QB	6-3	225	20/7/66	Wake Forest	NFL
11	Ellis, Todd	QB	6-2	211	16/5/67	South Carolina	D2
79	Erhorn, Oliver	LB	6-2	281	28/4/70	(Germany)	DIS
81	Farr, Mel	TE	6-0	237	12/8/66	UCLA	D5
	Flenoid, Bob	CB	5-11	182	17/8/67	Cal State – Long Beach	ORL
26	Floyd, Victor	RB	6-0	214	24/1/66	Florida State	D3
54	Forsythe, Byron	G	6-3	291	27/12/66	Houston	D10
20	Frazier, Paul	RB	5-8	197	12/11/67	Northwestern Louisiana	D1
88	Gaiters, Chris	WR	5-11	178	12/12/67	Minnesota	NY
45	Gerhart, Tom	S	6-0	191	4/6/65	Ohio	D11
5	Guidry, Mickey	QB	6-2	205	9/8/66	Louisiana State	EA
24	Hall, Mike	CB	6-0	194	14/1/65	New Mexico State	D12
52	Henton, Anthony	LB	6-1	218	27/7/63	Troy State	S1
96	Hill, Nate	DE	6-3	327	21/2/66	Auburn	D2
80	Holloway, Derek	WR	5-6	160	17/8/61	Arkansas	FA
	Huff, Richard	S	5-11	186	19/1/68	Yale	LON
77	Knight, Shawn	DE	6-6	292	4/6/64	Brigham Young	D1
57	Lindholm, Matti	LB	6-4	230	28/10/62	(Finland)	DIS
29	Malone, Art	CB	5-10	177	21/8/66	Washington	D8
21	McWright, Robert	CB	5-8	164	10/11/66	Texas Christian	D1
56	Moore, Tim	LB	6-3	216	1/1/65	Michigan State	D4
58	Najarian, Pete	LB	6-2	232	22/12/63	Minnesota	D1
8	Nies, John	P	6-0	195	13/2/64	Arizona	D1
75	Nua, Mark	T	6-6	330	12/12/64	Hawaii	D1
86	Parker, Carl	WR	6-2	210	5/2/65	Vanderbilt	D4
22	Perry, Leon	RB	6-1	233	16/10/66	Oklahoma	D6
76	Robb, Doug	C	6-3	283	12/12/66	Montclair State	FA
74	Salo, Juha	OL	6-3	290	11/8/66	(Finland)	DIS
71	Sapolu, Saute	DE	6-3	250	22/8/65	Arizona State	D3
58	Soltis, Paul	LB	6-2	232	1/10/66	Youngstown State	D6
62	Stephens, Richard	T	6-7	308	1/1/65	Tulsa	D2
87	Sumner, Colin	WR	6-3	188		California-Davis	LON
95	Thompson, Steve	LB	6-4	234	13/12/67	California-Davis	BAR
25	Wallace, Michael	CB	5-11	182	28/8/66	Jackson State	D10
51	Wilson, Curtis	C	6-3	273	30/10/65	Missouri	D3
59	Zumwalt, Rick	LB	6-2	231	19/5/65	Arizona State	D2

Roster correct at end of 1991 season. Key to How Acquired column: D1 – first round draft pick; S1 – first round pick in supplementary draft; FA – free agent; DIS – Operation Discovery; NFL – NFL enhancement allocation; EA – extra allocation draft; ORL – formerly with Orlando; NY – formerly with New York-New Jersey; LON – formerly with London; BAR – formerly with Barcelona.

SAN ANTONIO RIDERS

Address Texas Football Inc., 16404 San Pedro, Suite 240, San Antonio, TX 78232

Stadium Bobcat Stadium, San Marcos (capacity 23,000)

General Manager John Peterson

Head Coach Mike Riley

Team Colours Brown, metallic gold, orange, blue and scarlet

1991 record 4–6 (2nd in North American West Division)

SCOUTING REPORT Mike Riley leads the San Antonio Riders into the 1992 season with a solid foundation on which to build. The Riders missed the play-offs, but a third-place finish in the offensive rankings and fourth in the defensive standings are proof that there is potential here for Riley to work with. In the final analysis, the Riders' failure to capture the North American Division West title was down to their 16–12 loss in Week Six to the Birmingham Fire, who finished one win ahead of San Antonio despite trailing them in both offensive and defensive rankings. The decisive game at Legion Field was, in fact, a microcosm of the Riders' season; they outgained the Fire but lost the game because of a safety resulting from a bad snap, and four interceptions.

The Riders' passing game was the weakest area of their play all season and Riley should have been looking for a quarterback to provide missing leadership in this year's draft. Mike Johnson's 45.2 completion percentage was the lowest among the league's 10 number one quarterbacks, and his 10 interceptions, compared to just six touchdown passes, contributed to a poor rating of 54.3. Jason Garrett, from whom Johnson won the starting job, was more solid (a 71.0 rating), but was mostly unspectacular, averaging just 5.39 yards per attempt and managing only three touchdown throws. Neither man appears to have the qualities required to lift the Riders passing game higher than their 1991 ranking of seventh, particularly without a game-breaking receiver in their ranks and an offensive line which allowed more sacks (34) than they would have liked. That San Antonio were able to rank so high in total offense was due to their prolific rushing attack, which averaged a league-high 123.8 yards per game at a rate of 4.5 yards per attempt – second best in the

Quarterback Jason Garrett (3), sacked here by London, suffered behind a shaky offensive line.

league. Ricky Blake finished as the league's third leading rusher with 554 yards, even though his late-season productivity was reduced by injury and he carried the ball on average only 12 times a game. Undra Johnson and Broderick Graves played valuable supporting roles, but the Riders will need Blake to return from his NFL sojourn with the Dallas Cowboys – or to discover a similar talent in the draft – if they are to repeat the success of their ground attack during the 1992 season.

Defensively, the Riders were a difficult proposition; only three teams gave up fewer yards during last season. They allowed 3.7 yards per rushing attempt, the second lowest figure in the league, and their pass defense ranked second in yardage. Inside linebacker Tim Walton was a big factor in both of those statistics, shoring up the heart of the defense when opponents ran at them and breaking out of his confined quarters to create havoc in the offensive backfield with seven sacks when opponents attempted to take to the air.

San Antonio's special teams were among the best and worst. Their return units finished with only one team ranked lower on both kick-offs and punts, but their coverage teams were tough to penetrate. Their opponents' 5.9 yard average on punt returns was the league's lowest. Kent Sullivan proved an adequate punter, but the Riders need to find themselves a consistent place-kicker this year. They began 1991 with the Houston Oilers' Teddy Garcia, but cut him after he missed three out of four field goals – he was discarded during the summer by Houston, as well. Jim Gallery took over, but succeeded on just seven of 13 attempts, including missing all five kicks of 40-plus yards.

HEAD COACH Mike Riley was already a proven winner in professional football when he took the San Antonio job, having been head coach of two Grey Cup winning teams with the Canadian Football League's Winnipeg Blue Bombers in 1988 and 1990. The Blue Bombers reached the play-offs during each of his four years in charge, beating the British Columbia Lions in the 1988 final and the Edmonton Eskimos 50–11 in 1990. His 12–6 record in 1987 was the best by a CFL rookie head coach for 30 years. A former safety at the University of Alabama, who won the Southeastern Conference in each of his four years there, Riley began his coaching career as a graduate assistant at the University of California in 1975 and Whitworth College in 1976. He then coached the defensive secondary for six years at Linfield College, in Oregon, helping them win the NAIA national championship in 1982. From 1983 to 1985 he was defensive secondary coach at the Blue Bombers, and after a season as defensive coordinator at the University of Northern Colorado he returned to Winnipeg as head coach.

PASSING	Att	Cmp	Yds	Cmp%	Yds/Att	TD	TD%	Int	Int%	Lng	Rating
Johnson, M.	177	80	1137	45.2	6.42	6	3.4	10	5.6	82t	54.3
Garrett, Ja.	113	66	609	58.4	5.39	3	2.7	3	2.7	43t	71.0
Saltz	50	23	341	46.0	6.82	1	2.0	1	2.0	49	67.2
Bennett*	26	9	60	34.6	2.31	0	0.0	2	7.7	14	11.4
Williams	1	0	0	0.0	0.00	0	0.0	0	0.0	0	39.6
TEAM	341	169	2087	49.6	6.12	10	2.9	14	4.1	82t	61.6

RUSHING	No	Yds	Avg	Lng	TD
Blake	120	554	4.6	26	5
Johnson, U.	76	258	3.4	17	2
Graves	37	190	5.1	24t	2
Johnson, M.	28	185	6.6	22	0
Saltz	4	32	8.0	20	0
Hess	1	12	12.0	12	0
Garrett, Ja.	7	7	1.0	6	0
Bennett*	1	0	0.0	0	0
Sullivan	1	0	0.0	0	0
TEAM	271	1238	4.5	26	9

INTERCEPTIONS	No	Yds	Avg	Lng	TD
Nicholson	3	23	7.7	19	0
Lee	2	29	14.5	18	0
Watson	2	17	8.5	13	0
Cooney	2	14	7.0	14	0
Cheattom†	1	37	37.0	37	0
Wilson	1	23	23.0	23	0
Gilbert†	1	15	15.0	15	0
TEAM	12	158	13.2	37	0

RECEIVING	No	Yds	Avg	Lng	TD
Williams	30	321	10.7	34	0
Hess	28	399	14.3	37	2
Morris	23	409	17.8	73t	2
Garrett, Ja.	23	386	16.8	49	3
Pickens	20	249	12.5	82t	2
Blake	16	107	16.7	24	1
Graves	10	82	8.2	14	0
Johnson, U.	10	55	5.5	12	0
Searcy	5	52	10.4	20	0
Darrington	3	23	7.7	10	0
Hylliermark	1	4	4.0	4	0
TEAM	169	2087	12.3	82t	10

SACKS

Walton 7; Ledbetter 6; Manning 5; Gardner 3; Ross 3;
Wilson 2; Bailey 1.5; Cooks 1.5; Fletcher† 1; Snelson† 1.
TEAM: 31

KICKING	FG1-19	20-29	30-39	40-49	50+	PAT	Pts
Gallery	0/0	2/2	5/6	0/4	0/1	12/12	33
Garcia†	0/0	1/1	0/1	0/1	0/1	4/5	7
Rueda	0/0	0/0	0/0	0/0	0/0	2/2	2
TEAM	0/0	3/3	5/7	0/5	0/2	18/19	42

PUNTING	No	Yds	Avg	Net	TB	In20	Lng	Blk
Sullivan	59	2256	38.2	34.7	6	13	74	0

PUNT RETURNS	Ret	Fc	Yds	Avg	Lng	TD
Searcy*	28	4	127	4.5	16	0
Morris	8	6	30	3.8	13	0
Pickens	3	0	42	14.0	19	0
TEAM	33	8	183	5.5	19	0

● 1991 RESULTS ●

Mar 25	at Orlando	L	34–35	(21,714)
Apr 1	Frankfurt	L	3–10	(18,432)
Apr 7	Sacramento	W	10–3	(6,772)
Apr 15	at Raleigh-Durham	W	37–15	(13,500)
Apr 20	Barcelona	W	22–14	(16,500)
Apr 29	at Birmingham	L	12–16	(8,000)
May 6	London	L	15–38	(12,328)
May 11	at Barcelona	L	7–17	(23,670)
May 19	Montreal	W	27–10	(20,234)
May 25	at New York-New Jersey	L	9–38	(32,857)

KICK-OFF RETURNS	No	Yds	Avg	Lng	TD
Johnson, U.	14	305	21.8	36	0
Searcy*	13	260	20.0	30	0
Hess	8	137	17.1	31	0
Graves	3	47	15.7	22	0
Pickens	3	63	21.0	32	0
Williams	2	-4	-2.0	0	0
Manning	1	0	0.0	0	0
Morris	1	12	12.0	12	0
TEAM	41	727	17.7	36	0

● 1992 SCHEDULE ●

Sun, Mar 22	Montreal
Sun, Mar 29	at Birmingham
Sat, Apr 4	at New York-New Jersey
Sat, Apr 11	at Sacramento
Sun, Apr 19	Ohio
Sat, Apr 25	Birmingham
Sun, May 3	Orlando
Sun, May 10	at Barcelona
Sat, May 17	at Frankfurt
Sat, May 23	Sacramento

*Stats for Sacramento and San Antonio
†Not on roster at end of season

SAN ANTONIO RIDERS
roster

No	Name	Pos	Ht	Wt	Born	College	How Acqd
93	Bailey, David	DE	6-4	255	3/9/65	Oklahoma State	D2
5	Bennett, Ben	QB	6-1	199	5/5/63	Duke	SAC
72	Bjorkman, Stefan	DE	6-3	250	30/4/65	(Sweden)	DIS
23	Blake, Ricky	RB	6-2	235	15/7/67	Alabama A&M	D3
73	Collins, Sam	G	6-5	283		Baylor	FA
50	Cooks, Terrence	LB	6-0	230	25/10/66	Nicholls State	D3
28	Cooney, Anthony	S	6-1	203	8/2/67	Arkansas	D6
87	Darrington, Charlie	TE	6-2	224	23/6/66	Kentucky	D2
6	Gallery, Jim	K	6-1	214	15/9/61	Minnesota	D1
96	Gardner, Donnie	DE	6-3	260	17/2/68	Kentucky	D3
3	Garrett, Jason	QB	6-2	195	28/3/66	Princeton	D1
88	Garrett, John	WR	5-11	172	2/3/65	Princeton	D2
65	Grant, Eddie	C	6-2	273	16/8/67	Arizona State	D3
32	Graves, Broderick	RB	5-11	202	7/4/68	Winston-Salem	D2
77	Harper, James	G	6-2	289	6/9/66	Alcorn State	D1
83	Hess, Bill	WR	5-8	171	6/2/66	Westchester	D4
41	Hylliermark, John	S	6-1	205	11/11/64	(Sweden)	DIS
10	Johnson, Mike	QB	6-1	188	2/5/67	Akron	MON
27	Johnson, Undra	RB	5-10	204	8/1/66	West Virginia	D1
71	Kiselak, Mike	G	6-3	287	9/3/67	Maryland	D4
61	Layfield, John	G	6-5	278	29/11/68	Abilene Christian	D11
94	Ledbetter, Mike	LB	6-3	239	14/12/66	Washington State	D8
29	Lee, Greg	S	6-0	202	15/1/65	Arkansas State	D5
53	Little, Derrick	LB	6-3	250	1/12/66	South Carolina	MON
58	Manning, Roderick	LB	6-1	228	15/5/67	North Texas State	D2
86	Morris, Lee	WR	5-10	173	14/7/64	Oklahoma	D8
25	Nicholson, Calvin	CB	5-9	181	9/7/67	Oregon State	NFL
78	Ohrvall, Stefan	NT	6-3	247	3/12/62	(Sweden)	DIS
84	Pickens, Dwight	WR	5-10	177	18/5/66	Fresno State	D1
44	Richard, Gary	CB	5-10	173	14/7/64	Pittsburgh	D2
99	Ross, Gregory	DE	6-3	271	11/1/67	Memphis State	S7
21	Royal, Rickey	CB	5-9	186	26/7/66	Sam Houston State	LON
5	Rueda, Marco Antonio	K	5-11	188	8/1/64	(Mexico)	DIS
11	Saltz, Lee	QB	6-0	189	25/9/63	Temple	LON
80	Searcy, Elliott	WR	5-8	168	18/9/67	Southern	SAC
1	Sullivan, Kent	P	5-10	197	15/5/64	California Lutheran	D1
67	Vitale, John	C	6-0	262	28/12/65	Michigan	D6
54	Walton, Tim	LB	6-0	237	1/7/66	Ball State	D4
24	Watson, Ken	CB	6-1	185	10/11/66	Livingston	S2
82	Williams, Ronnie	TE	6-3	221	19/1/66	Oklahoma State	D1
46	Wilson, Kennedy	S	6-1	228	23/8/63	Purdue	D10

Roster correct at end of 1991 season. Key to How Acquired column: D1 – first round draft pick; S2 – second round pick in supplementary draft; DIS – Operation Discovery; NFL – NFL enhancement allocation; FA – free agent; SAC – formerly with Sacramento; MON – formerly with Montreal; LON – formerly with London.

OHIO GLORY

EXPANSION TEAM

Stadium Ohio Stadium (capacity 71,000)
General Manager Peter Hadhazy
Team Colours Royal blue, Nevada red and white

THE city of Columbus, Ohio, became the site of the World League's first expansion team when it was named late last November to take the place of the now-defunct Raleigh-Durham Skyhawks. Skyhawks owner George Shinn, a successful North Carolina businessman responsible for the Charlotte Hornets' entrance to the National Basketball Association, decided to cease operations after a disastrous 1991 season in which his team failed to win a game, averaged only 12,066 in attendance and cost him an awful lot of money.

The experience of trying to establish a team in a small media market in traditional basketball territory – compared to the success of the big-city teams in America and Europe – persuaded World League officials to place their new team in a larger market in proven football country. Columbus is the largest city in the seventh largest state in America, a state which boasts the NFL's Cleveland Browns and Cincinnati Bengals as well as a rich history in college football. It ranks among the top 25 markets in the country with a metropolitan population of 1.4 million. Although the Columbus franchise is a replacement for Raleigh-Durham, it is a true expansion franchise, the playing staff having been selected from scratch at this year's draft in Orlando, rather than having been inherited from the Skyhawks. The man chosen to guide the club's fortunes as general manager is Peter Hadhazy, a former executive vice-president of the Cleveland Browns and director of operations for the United States Football League. At the time of writing, their coaching staff and roster were unknown.

However, to complete the historical record of the World League's inaugural season, we are printing here the final player roster and 1991 individual statistics of the Raleigh-Durham Skyhawks, who are destined to become the subject of a sporting trivia question about the least successful team in professional American football history.

● Bobby McAllister, the Skyhawks quarterback, spent most of the 1991 season running for cover.

● Ohio hope to have more success than the Skyhawks, who ran into trouble against London.

PASSING	Att	Cmp	Yds	Cmp%	Yds/Att	TD	TD%	Int	Int%	Lng	Rating
McAllister	195	91	1152	46.7	5.91	7	3.6	11	5.6	72	54.0
Pizzo	88	36	629	40.9	7.15	2	2.3	5	5.7	62	49.9
Maye†	33	15	158	45.5	4.79	0	0.0	2	6.1	42	34.7
Burch	1	0	0	0.0	0.00	0	0.0	0	0.0	0	39.6
TEAM	317	142	1939	44.8	6.12	9	2.8	18	5.7	72	50.7

RUSHING	No	Yds	Avg	Lng	TD
McGill	38	187	4.9	31	0
Lowery	59	163	2.8	14	0
Burch	65	149	2.3	13	4
McAllister	26	106	4.1	22	1
Doctor†	17	49	2.9	14	1
Pizzo	10	39	3.9	11	1
Seay	2	28	14.0	30	0
Hargrove	1	18	18.0	18	0
Hines	3	8	2.7	4	0
Maye†	2	2	1.0	2	0
Meerten†	1	–1	–1.0	–1	0
TEAM	224	748	3.3	31	7

INTERCEPTIONS	No	Yds	Avg	Lng	TD
McGuirk	6	60	10.0	34	0
Samuel	3	6	2.0	6	0
Stedman	1	10	10.0	10	0
Jackson	1	3	3.0	3	0
Wilkinson	1	3	3.0	3	0
Ammons	1	0	0.0	0	0
Mack	1	0	0.0	0	0
TEAM	14	84	6.0	34	0

SACKS

Gadson 4; Carter 3; Riggins 3; Woodson 3; Grabisna 1; Jackson 1; Stedman 1. **TEAM: 16**

KICKING	FG1-19	20-29	30-39	40-49	50+	PAT	Pts
Hoyle	1/1	0/0	2/3	1/2	0/1	11/13	23

PUNTING	No	Yds	Avg	Net	TB	In20	Lng	Blk
Faunce†	27	996	36.9	28.2	4	3	47	1
Busch	40	1329	33.2	28.7	0	2	46	0
TEAM	68	2325	34.2	28.5	4	5	47	1

RECEIVING	No	Yds	Avg	Lng	TD
Hargrove	38	424	11.2	38	2
Hines	31	614	19.8	61	3
Doctor†	16	177	11.1	35	1
Seay	14	142	10.1	42	1
Burch	10	71	7.1	29t	1
Sprinkles	7	108	15.4	62	0
Johnson	6	122	20.3	30	1
Lowery	6	26	4.3	14	0
Meerten†	5	89	17.8	41	0
McGill	5	40	8.0	20	0
Patterson	4	126	31.5	72	0
TEAM	142	1939	13.7	72	9

PUNT RETURNS	Ret	Fc	Yds	Avg	Lng	TD
Hargrove	11	5	95	8.6	41	0
Johnson	3	0	18	6.0	10	0
Samuel†	1	0	0	0.0	0	0
Seay	1	0	0	0.0	0	0
TEAM	16	5	113	7.1	41	0

KICK-OFF RETURNS	No	Yds	Avg	Lng	TD
Hargrove	12	196	16.3	27	0
Seay	12	199	16.6	26	0
Johnson	9	193	21.4	29	0
Lowery	9	198	22.0	40	0
Burch	3	50	16.7	20	0
McGill	2	34	17.0	20	0
Samuel	2	38	19.0	21	0
Hines	1	24	24.0	24	0
Mack	1	22	22.0	22	0
Sprinkles	1	11	11.0	11	0
Woodson	1	10	10.0	10	0
TEAM	53	975	18.4	40	0

● 1991 RESULTS ●

Mar 23	at Sacramento	L	3–9	(15,126)
Mar 30	at Orlando	L	20–58	(20,811)
Apr 6	Barcelona	L	14–26	(19,656)
Apr 15	San Antonio	L	15–37	(13,500)
Apr 20	at Frankfurt	L	28–30	(21,065)
Apr 28	at London	L	10–35	(33,997)
May 5	New York-New Jersey	L	6–42	(10,069)
May 13	at Montreal	L	6–15	(20,123)
May 20	Orlando	L	14–20	(4,207)
May 25	Birmingham	L	7–28	(16,335)

*Stats for Sacramento and San Antonio
†Not on roster at end of season

RALEIGH-DURHAM SKYHAWKS roster

No	Name	Pos	Ht	Wt	Born	College	How Acqd
73	Ammons, David	DL	6-2	301	29/7/67	South Carolina State	D8
22	Aslaksen, Nicolay	RB	6-0	200	30/4/67	(USSR)	DIS
21	Burch, John	RB	5-10	209	4/1/66	Tenn-Martin	D3
1	Busch, Peter	QB	6-3	200	18/11/64	(Australia)	DIS
94	Butts, Anthony	NT	6-3	285	12/8/66	Mississippi State	D3
75	Carter, Jon	DE	6-4	292	23/4/65	Grambling State	D1
95	Estes, Mike	DE	6-4	276		Central Washington	BAR
52	Gadson, Ezekiel	LB	6-0	222	13/5/66	Pittsburgh	D1
54	Georgiev, Vladimir	LB	6-3	252	15/9/69	(USSR)	DIS
61	Glasson, Steve	LB	6-3	244	1/1/67	Illinois	D5
77	Grabisna, Erwin	DL	6-2	276	27/8/66	Case-Western Res.	D5
64	Gray, Terry	G	6-1	280	25/5/68	Baylor	D10
80	Hargrove, Marvin	WR	5-9	174	23/4/69	Richmond	D2
78	Henke, Brad	G	6-3	284	10/4/67	Arizona	D1
84	Hines, Clarkston	WR	5-11	163	21/3/67	Duke	S1
3	Hoyle, Wilson	K	5-10	167	6/12/66	Wake Forest	D2
47	Jackson, Ray	S	5-11	197	11/1/66	Ohio State	D4
89	Johnson, Andre	WR	5-9	164	8/12/67	Ferris State	D1
60	Kuipers, Jason	G	6-2	270		Florida State	FA
30	Lowery, Bren	RB	5-10	203	29/5/67	Maryland	D2
29	Mack, Gerald	CB	6-1	185	26/9/67	North Carolina Central	D5
11	McAllister, Bobby	QB	6-2	211	3/1/66	Michigan State	D2
20	McGill, Darryl	RB	5-10	207	8/3/66	Wake Forest	D4
26	McGuirk, Pat	CB	5-10	174	22/7/67	California Poly	D8
23	McPhatter, Brian	S	6-1	213		East Carolina	D6
8	Montgomery, Shane	QB	6-0	209	14/3/67	North Carolina State	D2
51	Myers, Woody	OL	6-4	259	23/12/64	South Carolina	D9
86	Patterson, Melvin	WR	6-1	190	7/9/65	Stephen F. Austin State	BIR
6	Pizzo, Joe	QB	6-1	217		Mars Hill	BIR
56	Riggins, Quentin	LB	5-11	201	14/4/68	Auburn	D3
31	Samuel, Peda	CB	5-7	159	27/9/65	Kansas	D7
90	Sapego, Oleg	DE	6-4	245	29/7/67	(USSR)	DIS
74	Scott, Michael	G	6-4	281	29/4/65	Missouri	D4
82	Seay, Clarence	WR	5-9	177	11/8/67	Texas-El Paso	D1
85	Sprinkles, Kevin	TE	6-3	249	8/10/67	Texas Tech	D3
71	Stallings, Robert	T	6-4	270	23/1/64	Southern Mississippi	BIR
96	Stedman, Troy	LB	6-3	237	19/5/65	Washburn	D4
98	Wilkinson, Rafe	LB	6-2	227	28/12/65	Richmond	D6
59	Woodson, Shawn	LB	6-2	225	12/8/66	James Madison	D2
53	Wulff, Paul	C	6-3	273	25/2/67	Washington	D7

Roster correct at end of 1991 season. Key to How Acquired column: D1 – first-round draft pick; S1 – first round pick in supplementary draft; DIS – Operation Discovery; FA – free agent; BAR – formerly with Barcelona; BIR – formerly with Birmingham

4
LEAGUE LEADERS 1991

TOUCHDOWNS	TD	Rush	Rec	Ret	Pts
Williams, B., *Orl*	11	0	11	0	66
Wilkerson, *Ny/NJ*	11	7	4	0	66
Alexander, J., *Lon*	10	9	1	0	60
Parker, *Sac*	8	0	8	0	48
Carr, *Bar*	8	8	0	0	48
Horton, *Lon*	8	0	8	0	48
Baker, *Frank*	6	5	1	0	38
Blake, *SA*	6	5	1	0	36
Graham, *NY/NJ*	6	6	0	0	36
Smith, D., *Lon*	6	6	0	0	36
Taylor, *Bar*	6	0	6	0	36

KICKING	PAT	FG	Lg	Pts
Alexander, P., *Lon*	37/39	9/13	40	64
Manca, *Bar*	18/21	14/22	42	60
Baumann, *Orl*	24/26	10/16	48	54
Nittmo, *Mont*	12/13	13/18	50	51
Belli, *NY/NJ*	25/25	5/12	45	40
Trainor, *Sac–NY/NJ*	12/14	9/16	46	39
Gallery, *SA*	12/12	7/13	37	33
Lyle, *Birm*	15/15	5/10	43	30
Maslo, *Frank*	7/9	6/13	43	25
Hoyle, *R-D*	11/13	4/7	44	23
Nies, *Sac*	11/12	4/7	42	23
Whelihan, *Frank*	6/7	4/6	36	18
Garcia, *SA*	4/5	1/4	26	7
Rueda, *SA*	2/2	0/0	0	2

LEADING RECEIVERS

RECEPTIONS	No	Yds	Avg	Long	TD
Garrett, *Lon (RB)*	71	620	8.7	47	1
Williams, B. *Orl*	59	811	13.7	t42	11
Parker, *Sac*	52	801	15.4	41	8
Horton, *Lon*	43	931	21.7	t96	8
Turner, *NY/NJ*	41	629	15.3	52	1
Gilbreath, *NY/NJ*	40	643	16.1	46	1
Bell, *Birm (RB)*	40	347	8.7	t65	1
Baker, *Frank (RB)*	39	423	10.8	28	1
Johnson, *Frank*	38	635	16.7	59	4
Hargrove, *R-D*	38	424	11.2	38	2
Taylor, *B*	35	745	21.3	t81	6
Davis, *Bar*	34	461	13.6	40	3
Hines, *R-D*	31	614	19.8	61	3
Dunn, *Mont*	31	321	10.4	31	1
Riley, *Lon*	30	506	16.9	t62	4
Williams, *SA*	30	321	10.7	34	0
Lewis, *NY/NJ*	29	475	16.4	t64	2
Bouyer, *Birm*	28	456	16.3	t87	2
Hess, *SA*	28	399	14.3	37	2
Brinson, *Lon*	28	351	12.5	38	1

YARDS	Yds	No	Avg	Long	TD
Horton, *Lon*	931	43	21.7	t96	8
Williams, B. *Orl*	811	59	13.7	t42	11
Parker, *Sac*	801	52	15.4	41	8
Taylor, *Bar*	745	35	21.3	t81	6
Gilbreath, *NY/NJ*	643	40	16.1	46	1
Johnson, *Frank*	635	38	16.7	59	4
Turner, *NY/NJ*	629	41	15.3	52	1
Garrett, *Lon (RB)*	620	71	8.7	47	1
Hines, *R-D*	614	31	19.8	61	3
Riley, *Lon*	506	30	16.9	t62	4
Lewis, *NY/NJ*	475	29	16.4	t64	2
Davis, *Bar*	461	34	13.6	40	3
Bouyer, *Birm*	456	28	16.3	t87	2
Hargrove, *R-D*	424	38	11.2	38	2
Baker, *Frank (RB)*	423	39	10.8	28	1
Burbage, *NY/NJ*	419	22	19.0	49	1
Morris, *SA*	409	23	17.8	t73	2
Hess, *SA*	399	28	14.3	37	2
Garrett, Jo., *SA*	386	23	16.8	49	3
Brinson, *Lon*	351	28	12.5	38	1

LEADING PASSERS	Att	Comp	Comp%	Yds	Avg Gain	TD	TD%	Lng	Int	Int%	Rating
Gelbaugh, *Lon*	303	189	62.4	2655	8.76	17	5.6	t96	12	4.0	92.8
Erney, *Bar*	158	79	50.0	1186	7.51	8	5.1	t81	2	1.3	86.6
Graham, *NY/NJ*	272	157	57.7	2407	8.85	8	2.9	t64	8	2.9	84.6
Bell, *Orl*	325	181	55.7	2214	6.81	17	5.2	t75	14	4.3	76.4
Elkins, *Sac*	312	153	49.0	2068	6.63	13	4.2	t60	13	4.2	67.1
Perez, *Frank*	357	171	47.9	2272	6.36	13	3.6	59	17	4.8	60.8
Pease, *Birm*	182	85	46.7	922	5.07	5	2.7	t87	6	3.3	57.5
Johnson, M., *SA*	177	80	45.2	1137	6.42	6	3.4	t82	10	5.6	54.3
McAllister, *R-D*	195	91	46.7	1152	5.91	7	3.6	72	11	5.6	54.0
Proctor, *Mont*	224	107	47.8	1222	5.46	3	1.3	53	10	4.5	50.5

LEADING RUSHERS

LEADING RUSHERS	Att	Yds	Avg	Long	TD
Wilkerson, *NY/NJ*	117	717	6.1	74	7
Baker, *Frank*	199	648	3.3	26	5
Blake, *SA*	120	554	4.6	26	5
Harris, *Mont-Birm*	135	540	4.0	t41	3
Johnson, *Mont*	110	423	3.8	t20	1
Floyd, *Sac*	92	406	4.4	25	2
Alexander, J., *Lon*	87	391	4.5	t41	9
Bell, *Bar*	137	367	2.7	15	0
Palmer, *Bar*	93	358	3.8	22	2
Frazier, *Sac*	90	308	3.4	31	3
Smith, D., *Lon*	84	302	3.6	t28	6
Jones, *Orl*	68	288	4.2	20	2
Mitchel, *Orl*	42	281	6.7	58	3
Johnson, U., *SA*	76	258	3.4	17	2
Proctor, *Mont*	41	247	6.0	26	2
Rice, *Bar*	33	210	6.4	24	2
Bell, *Birm*	66	192	2.9	11	0
Graves, *SA*	37	190	5.1	t24	2
Perez, *Frank*	44	189	4.3	26	0
McGill, *R-D*	38	187	4.9	31	0

YARDS FROM SCRIMMAGE

	Total	Rushing	Receiving
Baker, *Frank*	1071	648	423
Wilkerson, *NY/NJ*	990	717	273
Horton, *Lon*	931	0	931
Williams, B., *Orl*	829	18	811
Parker, *Sac*	801	0	801
Taylor, *Bar*	741	–4	745
Garrett, *Lon*	695	75	620
Blake, *SA*	661	554	107
Gilbreath, *NY/NJ*	643	0	643
Johnson, *Frank*	635	0	635
Turner, *NY/NJ*	629	0	629
Hines, *R-D*	622	8	614
Mitchel, *Orl*	593	281	312
Floyd, *Sac*	592	406	186
Johnson, *Mont*	580	423	157
Harris, *Mont-Birm*	569	540	29
Bell, *Birm*	539	192	347
Riley, *Lon*	528	22	506
Alexander, J., *Lon*	482	391	91
Lewis, *NY/NJ*	475	0	475

PUNT RETURN LEADERS

	No	Yds	Avg	Long	TD
Tucker, *Orl*	18	373	20.7	t66	1
Henry, *Birm*	23	247	10.7	73	1
Shelton, *Mont*	25	228	9.1	t67	1
Parker, *Sac*	15	127	8.5	19	0
Alexander, *NY/NJ*	20	143	7.2	18	0
Brinson, *Lon*	31	181	5.8	24	0
Searcy, *Sac-SA*	28	127	4.5	16	0
Johnson, *Frank*	24	89	3.7	15	0

KICK-OFF RETURN LEADERS

	No	Yds	Avg	Long	TD
Painter, *Orl*	24	597	24.9	48	0
Cadore, *Mont*	14	327	23.4	56	0
Johnson, U., *SA*	14	305	21.8	36	0
Baker, *Frank*	14	296	21.1	34	0
Woods, *Bar*	13	263	20.2	29	0
Searcy, *Sac-SA*	13	260	20.0	30	0
Harris, D., *Mont*	22	338	15.4	28	0

LEADING PUNTERS

LEADING PUNTERS	No	Yds	Lng	Avg	TB	Blk	Ret	Ret Yds	In 20	Net Avg
Mohr, *Mont*	57	2436	58	42.7	5	2	37	330	13	34.0
Lilljedahl, *NY/NJ*	39	1651	62	42.3	4	1	25	246	9	33.1
Maggio, *Birm*	61	2558	57	41.9	7	0	36	223	19	36.0
Aguiar, *Bar*	49	2029	80	41.4	3	1	26	278	15	33.8
Criswell, *Orl*	46	1827	56	39.7	4	0	27	208	10	33.5
Horne, *Lon*	37	1432	56	38.7	4	4	16	112	11	30.2
Sullivan, *SA*	59	2256	74	38.2	6	0	15	89	13	34.7
Whelihan, *Frank*	49	1846	61	37.7	2	0	21	193	18	32.9
Launce, *R-D*	27	996	47	36.9	4	1	9	126	3	28.2
Busch, *R-D*	40	1329	46	33.2	0	0	25	181	2	28.7
Rainor, *Sac*	29	946	56	32.6	1	0	7	6	3	31.7

INTERCEPTION LEADERS

	No	Yds	Long	TD
Parker, *NY/NJ*	11	270	t46	2
Newton, *NY/NJ*	8	104	46	0
Dodge, *Lon*	6	202	62	2
Miller, *Birm*	6	193	t99	1
Hunter, *Birm*	6	72	t37	1
McGuirk, *R-D*	6	60	34	0
Adams, *Sac*	4	17	15	0
Goetz, *Bar*	4	7	4	0

SACK LEADERS

Lockett, *Lon*	13.5
Hart, *Lon*	10.5
Brown, *Lon*	7.5
Campbell, *NY/NJ*	7.5
Woods, *NY/NJ*	7.5
Alexander, *Frank*	7.0
Bryant, *Orl*	7.0
Clark, *Bar*	7.0
Naposki, *Bar*	7.0
Oliver, *Birm*	7.0
Walton, *SA*	7.0

TOTAL DEFENSE

	Total	Rushing	Passing
Frankfurt	2311	772	1539
London	2463	740	1723
New York-New Jersey	2559	858	1701
San Antonio	2606	981	1625
Barcelona	2859	803	2056
Birmingham	2872	990	1882
Sacramento	3178	1402	1776
Montreal	3298	936	2362
Raleigh-Durham	3390	1417	1973
Orlando	3613	1046	2567

TOTAL OFFENSE

	Total	Rushing	Passing
London	3806	991	2815
New York-New Jersey	3262	1010	2252
San Antonio	3110	1238	1872
Barcelona	3087	1132	1955
Frankfurt	3053	896	2157
Sacramento	2997	1006	1991
Orlando	2951	901	2050
Raleigh-Durham	2369	748	1621
Montreal	2289	1158	1131
Birmingham	2225	865	1360

TEAM STATISTICS

	1ST DOWNS				3RD DOWNS			4TH DOWNS		
	Tot	Rush	Pass	Pen	Made	Att	Pct	Made	Att	Pct
London	191	66	112	13	44	112	39.3	4	6	66.7
NY/NJ	186	57	108	21	35	120	29.2	2	9	22.2
Frankfurt	180	52	109	19	45	131	34.4	4	9	44.4
Orlando	177	54	111	12	35	116	30.2	3	9	33.3
Sacramento	172	58	99	15	34	131	26.0	6	15	40.0
San Antonio	166	65	86	15	40	140	28.6	5	14	35.7
Barcelona	161	72	84	5	47	129	36.4	7	13	53.8
Montreal	147	69	61	17	37	133	27.8	3	10	30.0
R-D	134	44	81	9	37	132	28.0	6	12	50.0
Birmingham	118	50	59	9	36	126	28.6	3	11	27.3

OPPONENTS STATISTICS

	1ST DOWNS				3RD DOWNS			4TH DOWNS		
	Tot	Rush	Pass	Pen	Made	Att	Pct	Made	Att	Pct
NY/NJ	140	45	85	10	35	135	25.9	10	16	62.5
Frankfurt	141	47	72	22	28	126	22.2	4	14	28.6
London	145	35	92	18	40	140	28.6	3	14	21.4
San Antonio	148	58	76	14	32	117	27.4	3	7	42.9
Montreal	154	47	95	12	33	123	26.8	4	8	50.0
Birmingham	156	59	84	13	36	115	31.3	4	8	50.0
Barcelona	159	44	106	9	43	127	33.9	2	10	20.0
Sacramento	192	93	85	14	48	136	35.3	3	8	37.5
R-D	195	86	99	10	42	117	35.9	4	10	40.0
Orlando	202	73	116	13	53	134	39.6	6	13	46.2

5

THE LONDON MONARCHS IN PROFILE

LARRY KENNAN

TO DISCOVER just what the World League triumph of the London Monarchs in 1991 meant to head coach Larry Kennan, you need only take a look at his fingers. The Super Bowl ring he won as an assistant coach at the NFL's Los Angeles Raiders in 1984 has given way to the World Bowl ring he earned when the Monarchs beat the Barcelona Dragons 21–0 at Wembley last June. 'When you get the chance to play in the top game at any level, the stakes are always high', says Kennan, a 26-year coaching veteran. 'I felt much the same way about the World Bowl as I did when the Raiders played the Washington Redskins. It was every bit as big as the Super Bowl, even more so, because we put our team together in just three months and were suddenly on the brink of a championship. We were playing to be the best in the World League.'

Six months earlier, Kennan had been working as offensive coordinator of the Indianapolis Colts with the likes of Eric Dickerson, one of the NFL's greatest ever running backs, and top quarterback prospect Jeff George. Kennan had joined the Colts following a one-year stint at the Denver Broncos after leaving the Raiders in 1987. Interested in the aims of the World League and keen to become a head coach again for the first time since he left Lamar University, Texas, in 1981, Kennan was interviewed for the Monarchs job by general manager Billy Hicks. Hicks recalls, 'As soon as I had spoken to coach Kennan I knew he was the kind of guy we were looking for and the type of coach it would be easy to work with.' By the end of the season Hicks was giving Kennan the credit for bringing together 40 players who had never met before and turning them into a tight-knit winning combination, despite the vast majority having been transplanted to an unfamiliar environment thousands of miles from home. 'What we have at the Monarchs a real family feeling,' says Hicks. 'Coach Kennan,

and all our coaches, is the kind of guy the players can talk to and relate to and he has really helped create a feeling of unity.'

A proponent of a wide-open, varied style of offensive football, Kennan promised the Wembley fans an exciting season and he certainly didn't disappoint them. Never one to lose his temper during matches or practice, preferring a quiet word to get his message across, he consistently brought the best out of his players and had, he says, 'the most fun I've ever had in football.' Despite the long hours and sleepless nights that went into creating a championship team, Kennan insists, 'Last season was a real joy. We had so many great moments and great plays. Building tradition is important in a new team and I feel that we accomplished that. The first time through anything you never know how things are going to turn out, but our team made me so proud by their achievements.'

'We all had a wonderful time during our stay in London. The people in England have been very gracious in accepting us and the Wembley fans are super – the best in the league.'

Kennan, naturally, believes the World League has a bright future – and is more than happy with its present state. 'The standard of play in this league is outstanding. I have a lot of faith in this thing. The only problems we have had have been because of the newness of the league.' However big the World League becomes and however many more rings Kennan collects, you suspect it will be the 1991 season which will remain closest to his heart. 'I think it was something we will all look back on someday and feel that we were a part of history,' he says. 'It is a great feeling to know that you are a pioneer in any endeavour. I can imagine how the people who started up the NFL felt several years later when it really took off and blossomed. I'm sure we will feel the same way about the World League.'

THE STAR PLAYERS

JEFF ALEXANDER

RUNNING BACK Jeff Alexander maintains he has going on a diet to thank for his mid-season transformation into a heavyweight force in the London Monarchs offense in 1991. The former Denver Broncos starter shed 12 pounds after a disastrous start to the season and spent the rest of the year eating up the yardage and gorging himself on a feast of touchdowns.

The first running back selected by the Monarchs, Alexander was expected to be a key figure. His pedigree included starting six games and scoring two touchdowns for the Broncos in 1989, which helped them towards the Super Bowl. But things quickly began going wrong for the big man from Louisiana. Looking slow-footed and lacking in confidence, Alexander fumbled the ball three times in the first two games, lost his position to David Smith and ended the first five weeks of the season with just 70 yards and one touchdown to his name. 'I had trouble holding on to the ball early in the season,' he admits. 'David Smith stepped in and did an excellent job, so as he had started off better he got the chance to run the ball a little more than I did. I was having a rough time so I tried to do something to keep my mind positive, something I could look at and feel proud of even though I was going through a tough period on the field. By losing weight I was trying to do something positive off the field.'

The Jeff Alexander who turned up to play in the sixth week of the season against the Raleigh-Durham Skyhawks looked a far different proposition. Having come down from 245 pounds to 232 pounds, he appeared a yard quicker into the hole cleared for him by his blockers and considerably sharper in both thought and actions. His 55 yards and one touchdown rushing, plus another touchdown when he held Stan Gelbaugh's pass in the end zone, signalled the arrival of the real Jeff Alexander. During the final five weeks of the regular season he totalled 321 rushing yards at an average of greater than five yards per carry, and scored eight touchdowns. During the three-week road

trip to the States, when Smith was nursing an injury, Alexander carried the load of the Monarchs' rushing attack by scoring six touchdowns in three games and gaining 128 yards in a crucial victory in New York. 'It was too bad for Smitty that he got hurt, but it gave me the chance to carry the ball more,' says Alexander. 'Once I got the opportunity to carry the ball I felt I could make things happen. I felt a whole lot quicker and more in shape after losing the weight, so I'm glad I took time out to do it.'

Alexander added another 123 yards in the Monarchs' semi-final victory over the New York-New Jersey Knights, and the determination he showed in turning his season around was fully appreciated by London head coach Larry Kennan. 'Jeff's a good player. He started slowly, but he's a real quality person and it was nice to see him do well. He was a little overshadowed by Smitty and Judd Garrett to start with and was a little bit down when he fumbled the ball, but he's a real pro, a real man. He worked hard to improve his quickness and speed and worked hard at his passing game.'

Alexander was left out by the Broncos on Super Bowl day in January 1990, costing him the chance to face the San Francisco 49ers in football's biggest game in his home state. He was eventually cut by Denver just before the 1990 NFL season and arrived at the Monarchs' training camp with a long lay-off behind him. 'Jeff was a little rusty early in the season and that made him tentative when he carried the ball,' explains Kennan. 'But once he got his confidence back he looked good. He's a big man and he's a real load going through that line. You appreciate seeing a guy like that get his rewards.'

Jeff Alexander break free on his way to scoring in San Antonio.

PHIL ALEXANDER

LIKE ANY soccer-mad schoolboy, particularly one with a father in the professional ranks, Phil Alexander grew up dreaming of playing at Wembley Stadium. What he didn't reckon with was that when his dream came true it would be as a kicker for London's very own professional gridiron team. In 1991 not many observers had counted on Alexander, a former Norwich City soccer player and England Under-18 captain, being voted the best in his position in the World League after signing up as part of the Operation Discovery programme. Surely those guys, the four non-American players assigned to each team, were just there to make up the numbers – a token gesture to appease the local fans. Even Alexander himself wondered about his role on the team after hearing that the Monarchs had drafted Max Zendejas, an experienced NFL player with the Washington Redskins and Green Bay Packers and part of a famous family of kickers. 'I knew I had my work cut out,' Alexander recalls. 'And I soon discovered I wasn't going to get a lot of help from Max. It is a cut-throat business and I was after his job. We didn't do a lot of socialising together, although I went out with him a couple of times.'

Seven days before the opening game of the season in Frankfurt Alexander was given the news that Zendejas had been cut from the squad and the kicker's job was to be entrusted to him. 'Max is a good kicker and I knew what he could do,' explains coach Larry Kennan. 'I wasn't sure what Phil could do but he'd shown himself to be a top-flight NFL kicker in training camp. With his background in soccer I knew he'd competed in some big games and, at 29, he was not just some young kid coming out to kick for the first time. I didn't think the pressure of the game would affect him.' Alexander kicked a 25-yard field goal in Frankfurt and a week later fulfilled his Wembley dream by landing a crucial 40-yarder with his team 7–0 down in the second quarter against New York-New Jersey.

His father a professional for Scottish club Motherwell, Alexander grew up playing soccer and was on Norwich's books with England goalkeeper Chris Woods and Everton defender Dave Watson. After being released by them he spent four years playing in New Zealand, winning a full international cap for that country against the Soviet Union. On his return to England, he played for semi-professional team Wokingham Town and 'for a bit of fun' became the kicker for the Farnham Knights, an amateur British gridiron team. He made a name for himself by kicking a British record 54-yard field goal and set his sights on a professional career, and was given a trial by the Chicago Bears before signing to play in the World League.

The success of the Monarchs meant Alexander never had the opportunity to make the kind of last-second kick which can make or break reputations, but his record of 37 out of 39 conversion attempts and nine out of 13 field goals made him the top kicker in the league, a status confirmed in the All-World League team voting. 'The way the season went was such that I never really had to make a critical kick, although there were some important ones, like the one in the first game against New York and when we were 10–0 down just before half-time in the first game against Barcelona.'

The biggest disappointment of the season for Alexander was missing attempts of 45, 42 and 51 yards in the semi-final against New York, which may have harmed his chances of an NFL place, although the Houston Oilers did offer him a trial during the summer. 'It just wasn't my day,' he recalls, 'although I hit the last one really well and it just drifted to the left. I was glad we won the game in the end because I would have hated the season to have ended on that note.' It would indeed have been a terrible injustice for this former schoolboy dreamer whose powerful right leg struck such a blow for American footballers all over Britain in 1991.

Phil Alexander, a former soccer player for Norwich City, fulfilled his dream of playing at Wembley.

DANA BRINSON

IT TOOK only a short while for general manager Billy Hicks to discover what kind of character the London Monarchs had acquired in Dana Brinson, their first selection in the World League's draft of wide receivers. 'Coach Kennan was closing the first Monarchs team meeting the day after the completion of the draft,' recalls Hicks. 'He asked if there were any questions. Dana was sat there, slumped forward over the back of his chair, looking like Michael Jackson with that black head scarf he always wears and he finally called out, real slow, "Yeh, I've got one. When we get to London are we going to meet Princess Diana?" The guy is so cool.'

Brinson's performances during the Monarchs' triumphant season proved no less memorable. With feet that can dance like his pop hero Jackson around opponents' tackles, he had been promised star billing by his coaches. Too dangerous to be restricted to one area of the game, Brinson was used as a receiver, rusher and kick returner, scoring a touchdown in each category and winning second-team honours in the All-World League voting. Five feet nine inches of pure flamboyance, Brinson has few worries about being in the spotlight. Not only did he play his college football in front of America's most fanatical crowd at Nebraska, but, as he rather needlessly explains, 'I love attention.'

'The London fans want all the excitement they can get and I am the type of player who can give that. But the way I play is not influenced by wanting to be noticed. My personality is somewhat flamboyant so that doesn't change because people are watching me. I could make a mistake and hurt the team.'

'If you see me dancing around in the backfield, I'm just doing what I can to make positive yardage. Sometimes it takes that to avoid opponents. There aren't any complaints from the coaches. When I start losing yards, then they can get on my back.'

Dana Demone Brinson, born and raised in Valdosta, Georgia, became the star running back at Valdosta High School, traditionally one of the leading teams in the country. He was given a scholarship by Nebraska, but played only two games in his freshman year after being struck down by meningitis. When healthy again, Brinson – nicknamed D-Rock by his Nebraska quarterback – set about proving himself as one of the country's leading college players. A neck injury in his final year affected his value in the NFL draft and it was not until the eighth round that the San Diego Chargers took a chance and selected the man who had left Nebraska as the university's greatest ever kick returner.

Brinson was putting together a promising rookie season with the Chargers when he suffered a shoulder injury that ended his San Diego career. The Atlanta Falcons took him to their 1990 training camp, but Brinson was still looking for a job when the Monarchs showed enough faith in his fitness and ability to make him an integral part of their offense and special teams. 'Actually, I think it's the special teams I enjoy most,' he explains. 'I know at that point that I'm going to handle the ball. It's still a team situation, but a lot depends on my ability to avoid so many people and get to the point where I want to be. It's kind of exciting, a real challenge.'

Brinson, who returned a kick-off 93 yards for a touchdown against Montreal and had two touchdowns on punt returns ruled out because of team-mates' indiscretions, admits, 'When I'm waiting for that ball to come to me I'm just thinking, "I hope that big guy misses me". Sometimes it's frightening. Sometimes you have returns set up so you know you'll get some blocking. Other times, when we are trying to block the kick, it's just me against their whole defense.'

The name D-Rock, Brinson explains, is indicative of the way teams have always been able to rely on him. The London Monarchs know they can turn to him to produce the type of plays that have Wembley on its feet. 'I look at the name D-Rock as being solid,' he says. 'If you have a person who is doing several different things he has to be solid to accomplish those things. If you've got a rock you can count on it. Whatever happens, the London fans can rely on me.'

Dana Brinson in flamboyant style.

DEDRICK DODGE

OF ALL the colourful characters who wear the London Monarchs' uniforms, few can match the exuberance and lust for life of the splendidly named Dedrick Dodge. From the moment the Monarchs got together in training camp to the time they boarded their aeroplanes back to the U.S. after their World Bowl victory, 'The Blade' – as he became known during his college career at Florida State University – was never lost for words. Dodge constantly proved in 1991 that his actions could speak just as loudly as his words, however, finishing the season with a team-leading six interceptions and 40 tackles from his free safety position. Two of those interceptions went for touchdowns to earn Dodge a place at free safety on the All-World League second team, selected by the league's head coaches.

There were plenty of quarterbacks and wide receivers around the league who were happy to vouch for the coaches' choice, such as New York-New Jersey quarterback Jeff Graham, who saw Dodge make two game-saving interceptions against him in Week Two at Wembley and return another interception for a touchdown in New York in Week Eight. And then there was the little matter of Dodge's two pick-offs against Graham in the semi-finals, which he followed with yet another interception in the Monarchs' World Bowl success against Barcelona. Or ask San Antonio Riders receiver Bill Hess about the devastating hit he received from Dodge in Week Seven. That is, of course, if Hess can remember anything about it. He finished up unconscious on the turf after trying to get on the end of a pass to the sideline and feeling the full force of Dodge's helmet. At the time, the Riders were winning the game, but Monarchs coach Larry Kennan recalls, 'Dedrick's hit set the tone for the whole game.'

London quarterback John Witkowski, who was a few feet from the incident, adds, 'It was the hardest hit I have ever seen.'

In successive weeks on the Monarchs' road trip to America, Dodge returned an interception 62 yards against San Antonio, took one 32 yards for a touchdown in New York, and then scored from 60

yards with another interception against Sacramento. No wonder Kennan says, 'Dedrick's combination of hard-hitting and ability to come up with the key interception make him perhaps the finest free safety in the World League. Three games in a row he came up big for us. The thing about Dedrick is that even though he plays defense, he has the ability to go all the way to the end zone every time he gets the ball in his hands. He and his colleagues on the "No Goal Patrol" were a big part of our success.'

One of Dodge's pet topics of conversation during the season was the lack of respect shown by opposition teams towards the all-conquering Monarchs. 'Everywhere we went people were talking bad about us,' he says. 'They would say how they wanted to beat us and this and that. We were the number one team in the league, they should give us a little respect instead of putting us down. But all teams do when they do that is put the fuse to the fire.' Dodge's love of a good argument with opponents earned him a visit to the sin bin in the Monarchs' first game in New York, but he insists it was a case of mistaken identity. 'I didn't do anything. They got the wrong man. Usually I'm running my mouth and they can get me a lot of times for unsportsmanlike conduct, but that time I wasn't doing anything. I was just standing there when some dude grabbed me. Then the referees said, "Number 33, out!", just like that. They probably looked at me in the crowd and figured I had to have something to do with it.' Dodge, who hails from New Jersey and earned a place on the roster of the Seattle Seahawks for the 1991 NFL season, gained his revenge in that game with his match-winning touchdown, giving him an excuse to proclaim in the locker room, 'They respect The Blade about now.'

Trust Dedrick Dodge to have the last word.

Dedrick Dodge felt the London Monarchs were not always given the respect they deserved during their triumphant 1991 season.

VICTOR EBUBEDIKE

VICTOR EBUBEDIKE arrived at the London Monarchs' 1991 training camp in Orlando, Florida, a determined and somewhat bitter 25-year-old. As the first player signed by the WLAF under their Operation Discovery scheme – designed to introduce non-Americans into the league – he not only had to live up to his billing as the most celebrated 'foreigner' among the 10 teams, but also had a point to prove to the National Football League's New York Jets.

In the summer of 1990, Ebubedike, a former athlete from Maida Vale, north London, stood on the threshold of becoming the first product of the British version of American football to join the ranks of the NFL. After establishing himself as the most dominant player during the early years of the sport in Britain, and helping the London Ravens become the number one team, Ebubedike contacted all 28 NFL teams in the hope of a trial and was eventually invited across the Atlantic by the New York Jets.

Britain had sent players to the NFL before – kickers like Mick Luckhurst, the lad from St Albans whose family took him to the States as a teenager. But this was the nearest the British gridiron scene had come to having one of its own students graduate to the professional class. With his body-builder's physique, sprinter's speed and masochistic love of hard work, Ebubedike caught the eye of the Jets and was invited to their full training camp. But, having given up his job as area manager of a security firm, disappointment followed as he was discarded by the Jets before even being fitted for his shoulder pads. 'The truth is, there was a lot of back-stabbing aimed at me because of being a Brit,' he explains. 'I was cut just before breakfast on the second day of camp. There was a knock on the door and it was one of the assistant coaches telling me I had been released. I hadn't even had the chance to unpack my stuff. There were some people at the club who thought I was joking when I told them I was going.'

In a dark mood of depression, Ebubedike admits he was in no mood to reflect upon the achievement of having spent even one day in an NFL camp only eight years after his introduction to the sport. 'I was very

down when I got back to England,' confesses the MVP of Great Britain's 1989 European Championship triumph. 'I thought about all the people who must have been laughing because I hadn't made it. There were plenty of people in the British game who thought I'd been getting too big for my boots. For a long time I didn't even want to leave the house and I said I didn't want to play any more, but when I got back in the gym I felt better and I knew the World League was coming.' Ebubedike was lifted by the atmosphere of mutual respect he discovered with the Monarchs. 'The American guys made it clear from the start that we Brits were part of the team.'

His team-mates' celebrations after he scored his historic touchdown at Wembley against Orlando Thunder – the first by an Operation Discovery player – demonstrated how much they wanted him to succeed. 'I was very proud of Victor,' said Monarchs running back coach Hue Jackson. 'He has been an excellent guy to coach. Victor never complained when he wasn't getting to play, he just kept working. You just love guys like that. You know, Victor could be as good as anyone in this league. He has toughness, speed and ability and he wants to be successful.'

Ebubedike finished the season averaging 5.3 yards on 12 carries, as well as being an outstanding special teams player. With that experience behind him he could be ready to make a far bigger impact on the World League in his second season. 'Victor worked his tail off every day,' says London head coach Larry Kennan. 'He has proved that the British guys are not just here as token players. He is a very talented and very tough guy.' Tough, maybe, but in his moment of glory at the end of the Orlando game, the softer side of Victor Ebubedike was there for all to see. A volunteer worker with both able and disabled children, Ebubedike headed for the seats behind the Monarchs bench and spent a few minutes chatting with a fan in a wheelchair. Then, as he was being interviewed on television in the locker room, came the moment which melted the coldest of hearts. His face broke into a huge smile as he saw someone enter the room. 'It's my mum,' he said, beckoning her over or an emotional embrace.

From somewhere deep inside her son's grasp came he tearful words of a doting mother. 'I love you. I'm o proud of you.'

The whole of the British American football world was proud, too, of their most famous son.

Running back Victor Ebudedike struck a huge blow for American football in Britain when he scored a historic touchdown in the London Monarchs' victory over Orlando Thunder in front of his home-town crowd at Wembley.

JUDD GARRETT

JUDD GARRETT had every reason to make a lot of noise about his performance during the 1991 World League season. Instead, the quiet man of the London Monarchs chose to continue his work in his usual unassuming manner, which was why hardly anyone noticed when he ended up catching more passes than anyone else in the league.

The sight of Garrett sliding out of the backfield to take pass after pass from Stan Gelbaugh quickly became a standard feature of the Monarchs offense. To opponents, Garrett was like toothache, nagging away with annoying gains of between five and 10 yards and almost never dropping the ball. A product of Ivy League college Princeton, where he majored in religion, Garrett – the youngest of three brothers playing in the World League – finished the season with 71 catches. Then he added touchdown receptions in both the semi-final victory in New York and the World Bowl success against Barcelona. In fact, he caught more passes than he spoke words of self-promotion, preferring others to sing his praises and not minding too much if they didn't bother. General manager Billy Hicks happily takes up Garrett's case. 'Judd was one of the unsung MVPs of the team, especially in our type of offense. He was the go-to guy, the possession receiver who helped make a lot of what we did possible.

'You don't only go to him because he has all the tools to fit that mould, but because he is a gritty guy. He took some hits you were sure would decapitate him, but he just got up with that dazed look of his and got on with the job. He always had the same expression, whether it was a hard hit or a soft one, so he never let on whether he was hurt or not.'

It was inevitable that Garrett should end up playing football for a living. His father is a former college head coach and his two brothers, John and Jason, preceded him at Princeton. Garrett finished his college career as the holder of all the school's rushing records, including yards (3,109), touchdowns (32) and all-purpose yardage (4,510). In his senior year he set another school record by rushing for 1,347 yards and was named the Ivy League Player of the

Year, as well as being selected as a second-team All-American by the Associated Press.

Garrett's brothers, quarterback Jason and wide receiver John, both ended up playing for the San Antonio Riders, while Judd was a second round draft pick by the Monarchs after catching the eye of Hicks and London head coach Larry Kennan during the work-outs that were held before the draft. 'All the Garrett boys were the kind of guys you love in that kind of situation,' says Hicks. 'They are precise football players and they executed everything they had to do perfectly. Growing up with a coach for a dad, they know the basics. Coach Kennan had a lot of film on Judd from his time in the NFL and we tagged him straight away as a second round pick if we could get him.'

Garrett was released by the Philadelphia Eagles and Dallas Cowboys before joining the Monarchs, and was turned down by the Buffalo Bills after playing for them in last year's American Bowl at Wembley, following his World League success. Garrett set the WLAF record for receptions in a game when he held 12 passes in the Monarchs' victory against Birmingham. But it is a performance that has been virtually forgotten. 'One of the things you love about Judd is that he is not a self-publicist, off the field or on it,' says Hicks. 'You would look back at games last season and think, "Oh, Judd had a pretty good game," and then you'd look at the stats and see that he actually caught about 10 passes and converted half a dozen third downs. Because of the way he is, the things he does out there on the field do not get burned into your memory.'

Judd Garrett is congratulated by Jon Horton after scoring in the Monarchs' semi-final win.

STAN GELBAUGH

WHILE MOST of the World League players were preparing for their first season, Stan Gelbaugh, the man who was to have probably the biggest impact on the league in its inaugural year, was selling fax machines. By the time the London Monarchs lifted the World Bowl trophy, their quarterback had carried off the league's Offensive MVP award and finished as the top-rated passer with league highs in yardage (2,655), completion percentage (62.4) and touchdown passes (17).

After five years of trying to find a steady job in football, Gelbaugh, at 28, had just about given up hope. Then the opportunity arose to add World League experience to a curriculum vitae which already included the NFL's Buffalo Bills and the Canadian Football League's Saskatchewan Roughriders, where he played as a punter. 'When I first heard about the league I was selling copiers and fax machines back home in Maryland,' says Gelbaugh. 'I didn't like the job but for the amount of money they were paying in the WLAF maybe it was just time to get on with my life. But I realised that I missed the game and decided to give it another shot. A friend of mine who is a defensive coach at Sacramento, Jim Haslett, called and asked if I wanted a job. I said okay and they put me in the supplementary draft. They had first pick but they passed me by and the Monarchs took me instead.' It turned out to be a costly mistake by Sacramento and a piece of good fortune for the Monarchs, who realised that, despite having already chosen a top-class quarterback in John Witkowski in the original draft, Gelbaugh was too good to ignore.

A slender six foot three inches, Gelbaugh would be unlikely to be picked out as an American footballer in a crowded room. In the hurly burly of life behind the line of scrimmage, however, he looked every inch the part. 'Stan played big-time,' according to Monarchs coach Larry Kennan. 'He proved to be a real field general. He showed real presence, real poise and made some incredible plays during the season.'

Gelbaugh could hardly have foreseen this particular turn in his career during his college days at Maryland, where he backed up Cincinnati Bengals quarterback Boomer Esiason and Buffalo's Frank Reich for three years. When he became a starter in his senior year, he showed NFL potential with 15 touchdown passes and just four interceptions. He was drafted by the Dallas Cowboys, which he admits was probably the worst thing that could have happened. 'My hero as I was growing up was Roger Staubach, the Cowboys quarterback. So when the Cowboys drafted me I wasn't really focussed on playing football. I was like a giddy little kid in the candy store. I wasn't ready to go out there and perform the way I can and the way they expected.'

Cut by the Cowboys, Gelbaugh punted in Canada before three unspectacular years at Buffalo and one training camp at the Cincinnati Bengals. But his success in the World League won him a place on the Phoenix Cardinals' roster for the 1991 season. He threw his first NFL touchdown pass, a 34-yarder, against the New York Giants and started three games. 'I certainly don't consider myself on a par with the stars,' says Gelbaugh when asked to compare himself with other NFL quarterbacks. 'I will never be a Joe Montana or Dan Marino. But when I see some of the guys out there I know I am as good as them or could be better if I was given their opportunities.' What is beyond dispute is that Gelbaugh was the pick of the World League's quarterback class of '91. And one lesson the season taught him is that there can be no going back to fax machines. 'After being out of sports and working in a regular job and then getting back into it, I realise how much fun sports are. I am going to stick with it, whether as a coach or whatever.'

London Monarchs quarterback Stan Gelbaugh carried off the World League's Offensive MVP award after a brilliant season in which he threw 17 touchdown passes and was the league's top-rated passer

ROY HART

CALL ROY HART the Quiet Assassin. Ask the London Monarchs' 21-stone nose tackle about his particular trade, the destruction of opposing quarterbacks and running backs, and he answers with a politeness and softness of voice that belies the ruthlessness of his words. From his position at the centre of the defensive line, Hart is in a position to almost smell the fear of a quarterback and he has a deadly gleam in his eyes when he describes, in a near whisper, the moment when he realises he has his prey cornered. 'Sometimes the quarterback will come up to the line and he will have a rattly voice and he will be trembling a little bit. He'll be shaking because he wants to get the ball from the centre and get out of there as quick as he can. He knows the rush is coming. If you can get him rattled you can destroy the offense. He is the guy who runs the whole offensive unit. Get to him and you've got half the job done.'

Hart's 10.5 sacks last season were second in the league to team-mate Danny Lockett, a remarkable feat for a player in his position, where more often than not he was faced with two blockers. 'My game is I love to penetrate, I love to make things happen, I love to dictate. Playing nose tackle, I am able to do that and those are the kind of things I concentrate on doing. Jim Washburn, the defensive line coach, allows me to have freedom to do some nice things.' The assaults he carried out on opposing players in 1991 – leading the Monarchs with 84 tackles – could hardly be described as 'nice'. But they gave the South Carolina graduate a chance to prove that the Seattle Seahawks were wrong to decide after two years that he was too small, at an even six foot, to play nose tackle in the NFL. 'The World League has given me the chance to show that Roy Hart is a quality football player and that I can play on any level given the opportunity. I have to thank the Monarchs for giving me the chance to do things that I never had the opportunity to do with the Seahawks and to be part of one of the best defenses in the league.'

Soft-spoken Hart may be in his street clothes, but put him in a football uniform and he becomes a great motivator of colleagues, happily assuming the role of inspirational leader of the 'Hart Attack Defense'. 'Playing nose tackle is a very tough position. You have to be aware of what is happening around you an I take on the position to the best of my ability in orde that my team-mates can see that I am giving it my all and playing 100 per cent. I hope they follow that because I like to lead by example. I talk sometimes and I get emotional, but I like to lead by my play, tha is the ultimate leader.'

The Monarchs' first draft choice among the defensive linemen, Hart made a big enough impression during their successful season that the Los Angeles Raiders signed him for the 1991 NFL season. However, after starting a pre-season game against the San Francisco 49ers, he was placed on the injured reserve list before the start of the regular season. At least it spared the NFL's offensive linemen having to stare across at the imposing figure of Hart and wondering what was running through his mind. As Hart explains, 'When I line up I am concentrating completely on what I have to do. I know who I have to get and how to get them, whether that person is the quarterback or the running back. I know who to go through and what direction I need to take to get it done.'

'The greatest satisfaction is to get to the quarterback because that is the ultimate. You are out there to stop that guy running the offense, to corrupt what he is trying to do. Get to him and it gives you a natural high.'

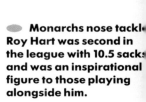

● Monarchs nose tackle Roy Hart was second in the league with 10.5 sacks and was an inspirational figure to those playing alongside him.

JON HORTON

IT IS one of the most enduring images of the London Monarchs' 1991 season; the six-foot one-inch figure of wide receiver Jon Horton reaching up like an extendable ladder, plucking the ball effortlessly out of the air, landing with the grace of a ballet dancer and finally gliding away to the end zone with defenders sprawled forlornly in his wake. From the moment Horton turned up on the end of quarterback Stan Gelbaugh's 96-yard touchdown pass in the opening game against Frankfurt, the Monarchs knew they could rely on Horton whenever they needed to make big yardage in quick time.

In compiling the most receiving yards in the league (931) at the highest average per catch (21.7), Horton boasted three touchdowns of longer than 30 yards among his eight scores. And against Sacramento in Week Nine he set the league's regular season record of 196 yards on just eight catches. But that was nothing compared to his play-off performances. In the Monarchs' semi-final victory in New York, Horton turned the game with touchdowns of 68 and 78 yards, before breaking the deadlock against Barcelona in the World Bowl with a superb 59-yard effort. 'The day we drafted Jon the coaching staff said he reminded them of John Taylor of the San Francisco 49ers with his ability to make the big play after the catch,' says Monarchs head coach Larry Kennan. 'Many of his touchdowns were perfect examples of that.'

Horton can be matter-of-fact in explaining his ability to make the big plays. 'Stan and I just click on those long ones,' he says. 'It seems like everybody knows where the ball is going and we are still able to pull it off.' But when pressed harder, Horton happily gives a seminar on the art of the wide receiver. 'The reason I am able to get to the ball before the defensive back is that I am hungry,' he explains. 'I have great desire. I seem to have that little knack of wanting the ball. Our receivers coach, Hue Jackson, tries to teach me to attack the ball at its highest point. That's what I try to do – go up and get the ball. My thoughts are either I am going to get the ball or nobody is going to get it.' Of all his spectacular touchdowns for the Monarchs, maybe the one that gave Horton most

pleasure was one that featured the simplest catch. With London holding a slender 28–26 lead over New York-New Jersey late in their semi-final, Gelbaugh tossed a short pass to Horton, who had to win a foot race against the Knights' defense to turn the play into a 78-yard score. 'There were a lot of doubters about my speed,' he said, 'so I was pleased to show them

at nobody was going to catch me. It is something I
ke pride in. I don't just want to be a speedster, I
ant to be known as a man who's aggressive and
kes no prisoners to get that ball, but it was nice to
ow I can run as well.'

Horton's athletic ability was rarely questioned
uring his college career at Arizona, where he

finished as the school's second leading receiver of
all-time with 114 catches for 2,389 yards and 15
touchdowns. It wasn't enough to earn him a place
with a professional team and he eventually ended up
playing a season of pro basketball in Mexico.
Released by the Canadian Football League's British
Columbia Lions and then by the San Francisco 49ers,
Horton had earned a reputation as a rather difficult
customer by the time the World League draft came
around last February. But the Monarchs could not
have been more delighted by the professionalism and
leadership shown by Horton during the season. 'I
guess you could say we took something of a chance on
Jon,' admits general manager Billy Hicks. 'He came
to us with a bit of a reputation. But I told him myself
how impressed I had been by the way he conducted
himself as a player and a person during the season.
He was the model professional.'

Horton, who married an English girl during the off-
season, also impressed the British media, who voted
him the Monarchs' Player of the Year. And even when
he wasn't catching passes himself, the threat he
posed to wary defenders helped his colleagues in the
Monarchs' receiving corps — the Bomb Squad — take
full advantage and turn their group into the most
feared in the league. It was the success of that unit
which gave Horton as much pleasure as his own
personal achievements. 'At the beginning I think it
was a kind of touchy thing between us,' he says of the
rivalry between himself and Bomb Squad members
Andre Riley, Dana Brinson and Tony Sargent. 'After
a while we didn't care who caught most passes. We
wanted everyone to do well. We just wanted to show
the city of London and the World League that we are
the best group.'

⬤ **Jon Horton was
chosen as the Monarchs'
Player of the Year by the
British media. Here, he
receives his trophy from
former World League
president Mike Lynn.**

DANNY LOCKETT

THE ONLY surprise concerning Danny Lockett's selection to the All-World League team at the end of the 1991 season was that he was not a unanimous choice among those picking the team, the league's head coaches. But then again, a lot of those men had a large grudge to bear against a player who had spent the entire season wrecking their offensive plans and inflicting pain on their quarterbacks. From his position at outside linebacker, Lockett was given a licence to kill by the Monarchs coaches – and the native of Fort Valley, Georgia, did just that to any number of opposition drives with his league-leading 13.5 sacks and a total of 46 unassisted tackles, as well as 13 quarterback pressures. Lockett was an explosion waiting to happen every time the opposing centre snapped the ball. He proved virtually impossible to block as he propelled his six-foot three-inch frame into the offensive backfield with a nimbleness of foot which contradicted his 18 stones. Not content with his regular season contribution – which earned him a third share of the league's Defensive MVP award – he added 2.5 sacks in the Monarchs' semi-final victory in New York and recorded four tackles and a fumble recovery in the World Bowl against Barcelona.

Another possible reason why Lockett did not win the unanimous approval of the coaches was that he made a few enemies during the season with his uncompromising style. Neither was he slow to let a quarterback know when he had got the better of him. 'Me and the quarterback had a few words sometimes,' he admits. 'I can get excited and get vocal, but in the end I don't let all the hype and stuff get to me. I have a job to do, to go out there and help us win a football game. The most important thing is how you put it together when you get out on the field, letting your actions speak for themselves.'

Lockett enjoyed an outstanding college career at Arizona, registering 21 sacks in two seasons and being awarded second team All-Pac 10 Conference honours in his senior year in 1986. He was then selected by the Detroit Lions in the sixth round of the 1987 NFL draft and celebrated his rookie season with 35 tackles and one sack in 12 games. He played in a 16 games of the 1988 season, but was released before the 1989 campaign and failed to win a job at the San Francisco 49ers a year later.

The second linebacker drafted by the Monarchs, Lockett immediately made an impact with five sacks in the first two games of the 1991 World League season. 'He can just take control of a game,' says London head coach Larry Kennan. 'He makes big play after big play on the field. He can cause havoc with a gameplan because he penetrates so well. I think he is the best defensive player in the World League without a doubt.' The New York Jets apparently agreed, signing Lockett soon after the Monarchs' World Bowl victory, but released him before the 1991 NFL season started. The Buffalo Bill also took a look at him, but decided not to utilise the talent which had been such a big part of the Monarchs' success.

While admitting that he desperately wants to play NFL football again, Lockett acknowledges the success he enjoyed last season in the Monarchs' defensive scheme. 'We play good defense,' he says. 'Most of the teams we played had a lot of mental breakdowns during games. That never happened to us. We always had players in the right place at the right time. Our coaches worked hard at that and that helped me have a successful season.'

● **Danny Lockett led the World League with 13.5 sacks last season and earned a share of the Defensive MVP award.**

THE NASTY BOYZ

ASK A general where victory in any battle begins, and he'll probably cite the men in the trenches. Ask London Monarchs coach Larry Kennan to name the starting point for his team's World League triumph and he will give you football's equivalent answer: the men on the offensive line.

The Monarchs were fortunate in having the most intimidating collection of grunts in the league, the Nasty Boyz. Weighing in at an average of almost 21 stones each and standing on average six feet three inches tall, there was no unit in the World League better at blasting holes in the opposition defensive line for their running backs to burst through, no set of minders more adept at keeping their quarterback safe from marauding linebackers. Of the five starters on the Monarchs offensive line, three – centre Doug Marrone, tackle Steve Gabbard and guard Paul Berardelli – were selected for the All-World League first team. Tackle Theo Adams was a second-team choice, while guard Larry Jones can consider himself desperately unlucky to have missed out on similar honours. Reserves Todd Oberdorf and John Fruhmorgen can simply count themselves unlucky to find themselves sharing a locker room with such a talented group.

Of all the positions on an American football field, it is the offensive line which carries the least prestige, the fewest headlines. So it says much for the Nasty Boyz that they became one of the most visible sections of the Monarchs team with their impressive list of achievements. During the season they allowed the fewest sacks of any team in the league. While Monarchs quarterbacks bit the dust only 10 times, the next best effort was that of the Frankfurt offensive line, who allowed 19 sacks. They helped the Monarchs launch 42 touchdown drives, averaging 57 yards and six plays each, while propelling their team to a league-best average of 31 points and more than 380 yards per game. There are no individual statistics to underscore the work of an offensive lineman, but Kennan is in no doubt about the worth of the Nasty Boyz. 'They are a talented bunch of guys who are smart and experienced,' he says. 'Our

quarterbacks had great pass protection all season. The grit and guile of these guys amazes me.'

'I don't even try to come up with superlatives for these guys any more. They just do the job day after day and week after week.'

As the first position to be dealt with in the World League draft, the offensive linemen were the first players to become London Monarchs. Gabbard came to the Monarchs via Florida State University and the

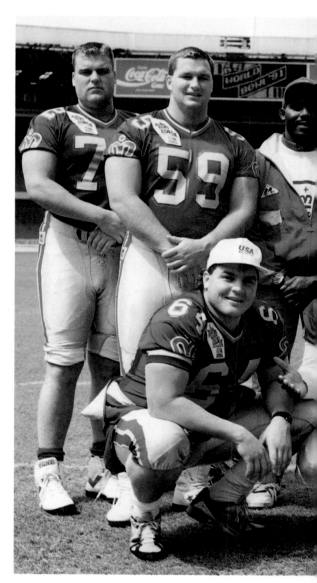

Philadelphia Eagles; Adams from the University of Hawaii and the Los Angeles Rams' training camp; Berardelli via Villanova and the Eagles; and Jones as a free agent from the University of Hawaii. It was Marrone who brought the most NFL baggage with him, having been drafted by the Los Angeles Raiders in 1986 and having spent spells at the Miami Dolphins, Dallas Cowboys, New Orleans Saints and Minnesota Vikings.

Self-discipline is vital to an offensive lineman, and it was self-discipline that helped the Nasty Boyz maintain their poise in the heat of some fierce trench warfare last season. Marrone explains, 'Sometimes you know it is going to be bad out there, that there is going to be some bad blood between you and the other team's defensive line. But that inspires me to not let anyone intimidate me. I'm too old and experienced to be intimidated and let things like that bother me. I just go out there to play good, hard football. I don't have to prove anything to anyone and I don't have to take any cheap shots at anyone.'

If the Nasty Boyz created havoc in opponents' defensive lines last year, it was nothing to the problems they caused at the Monarchs' headquarters at the United States International University, in Bushey, Hertfordshire. The beds in the players' rooms were simply too small for such giant specimens and the Nasties ended up having to be given two beds each to sleep on. It was also largely due to their need to keep their strength up that the Monarchs regularly consumed more food in a single day than the 296 students on campus put together. After all, armies – particularly the men in the trenches – do march on their stomachs.

● Meet the Nasty Boyz: Todd Oberdorf (72), Doug Marrone (59), Theo Adams (60), Steve Gabbard (67), John Fruhmorgen (64), Larry Jones (68) and Paul Berardelli (70). Pictured with the league's best offensive line is Monarchs offensive coordinator George Warhop.

ANDRE RILEY

IT WAS all going horribly wrong. After less than two quarters of their semi-final against the New York-New Jersey Knights, the London Monarchs were 17–0 behind. If they could get their offense into gear and score on the next drive, there was still hope. If they failed again and the Knights were given the chance to stretch their lead further, a season which promised so much could end in bitter disappointment.

What was required, in this key match, was someone to step forward and breath life into the Monarchs. Andre Riley, a tough little wide receiver with 30 catches to his name during the regular season, proved to be that man. First, he was safely on the end of a 38-yard pass from Stan Gelbaugh to put the Monarchs within striking distance of their first points. Then, with six yards needed for a touchdown, Riley set up camp inches inside the end zone, awaited Gelbaugh's pass and stubbornly refused to let the ball slip from his grasp as two defenders charged into him from behind in a violent effort to shake it loose. The Monarchs were back on the road to the World Bowl, and Riley's performance on that drive was certainly a candidate for the most decisive moment of the season. So often during the campaign, it was the dependable five-foot nine-inch figure of Riley to whom the Monarchs looked when they needed vital yards in tight situations. Very few of his catches came cheaply, most of them being made when the stakes were at their highest.

Already blessed with Dana Brinson and Jon Horton at the wide receiver positions after the original league draft, the Monarchs had no hesitation in adding to their strength when Riley became available in the supplementary draft a few days later. Once Tony Sargent had also been signed as a free agent, the Bomb Squad – a receiving corps which would explode in the faces of the league's defensive backs – was complete. Riley is the quietest, most serious member of the quartet. He holds the concept of four modern-day musketeers close to his heart and when it comes to publicity pictures of the Bomb Squad he has the most definite ideas about the best way for the unit to

be portrayed. 'These are the kind of guys I would be hanging out with wherever I was or whatever I was doing,' he says. 'Our characters are pretty similar and we all get along well, although we have different aspects to our personalities.

'We're pretty tight and we give each other support and confidence. Just by Jon doing well it gives me confidence, and so on.' With the Bomb Squad becoming a target for a lot of provocative comments from opponents last season, Riley warns, 'If you threaten one of us, you threaten all of us. We take care of each other.'

Riley, a native Californian, would be a handful for the opposition even without the help of talented colleagues. In 1989 he became the first Washington Huskies player to surpass 1,000 receiving yards in a season and his 53 receptions were just one shy of the school record. Already showing the happy knack of making big plays at important moments, 75 per cent of his catches produced first downs for his team. 'I used to know all about Andre when he was at Washington and I was coaching against him at Pacific,' says Monarchs running backs and receivers coach Hue Jackson. 'It's nice to have him on my side now. 1991 was the most fun season of my life, coaching guys like Andre and the Bomb Squad.'

It wasn't so much fun for the Monarchs defensive backs having to spend two hours a day chasing Riley and Co. around the practice field. Safety Dan Crossman explains, 'Andre runs such great routes. He is a tough kid who is going to block you on every play and be in your face the whole time. I think of him as a pest – he's right there in your hip pocket, pushing you and blocking you.'

Monarchs coach Larry Kennan concludes, 'We knew Andre was going to be a very good player for us when we picked him in the supplementary draft. He is everything we hoped he would be, maybe even better.'

Right: London Monarchs wide receiver Andre Riley holds the ball aloft to salute his team's opening touchdown in their semi-final victory against the New York-New Jersey Knights.

JOHN WITKOWSKI

JOHN WITKOWSKI had plenty of time to sit and dream of what might have been last season as he watched Stan Gelbaugh carry out the job for which he believed he had been chosen. The London Monarchs' first selection in the league's quarterback draft, Witkowski had every reason to expect that it would have been him leading them to the World Bowl, winning the World League Offensive MVP award and earning himself a shot at NFL stardom – and if events had taken a different course on the opening night of the season in Frankfurt, it easily could have been.

Witkowski, who came to London with NFL experience with the Detroit Lions behind him, knew he had a rival for the Monarchs quarterback job when Gelbaugh was selected in the first round of the supplementary draft. The two men were so evenly matched that head coach Larry Kennan chose to play them for one half each in the first game against Frankfurt Galaxy. Witkowski drew the short straw, playing the first half behind an offensive line who took time to get their game together. He left at half-time having been sacked three times and having completed just eight of 16 passes. Gelbaugh, receiving the protection Witkowski had been denied, threw a 96-yard touchdown pass and was never to lose his position. In fact, the Monarchs allowed only seven more sacks all season. 'That's football,' says Witkowski, whose only other meaningful appearance came in New York in Week Eight, when he replaced the injured Gelbaugh for the second half and led the Monarchs' only touchdown drive of the game. 'Stan made the most of his opportunity and did a great job all season. He deserved to be the starter and deserved to be the MVP.'

Witkowski's day could yet arrive, however, in 1992. With Gelbaugh's elevation to the NFL at the Phoenix Cardinals casting doubt over his return to the World League, Witkowski may find himself at the Monarchs' helm this season. At the age of 29, he possesses the experience and leadership coach Kennan values so highly – qualities most World League teams were sadly lacking from their quarterbacks last season. Indeed, Witkowski would probably have been the starter for all nine other teams. Selected in the sixth round of the NFL draft by the Lions in 1984, Witkowski was appointed offensive captain of the Monarchs last season and fully appreciates what is expected of a team's starting quarterback. 'The first thing you think about is that you have to be a leader,' he says. 'You have to go out there and take charge of the offense. Guys look up to you, you are the guy who is being vocal in the huddle and telling everybody what to do. Everything starts with you.' As was so evident in the first half in Frankfurt, Witkowski stresses, however, that a quarterback is only as effective as his offensive line. 'Without them nothing can be finished. A quarterback gets a lot of hype, but he is only as good as his linemen. He can't do his job if they don't get their job done.'

Witkowski, a New Yorker, attended Columbia University and was named Ivy league Player of the Year in 1982 before being signed by Detroit. He started one game during his rookie season, against the Chicago Bears, and had spells with the Houston Oilers and Green Bay Packers without ever getting into a game. 'I always thought I was in the wrong place at the wrong time,' he says of his NFL career – a statement which could equally be applied to his World League career so far. 'I used to bang my head against a wall thinking about things like that. I don't do it any more, I just go out and play football and leave the other guys to make the decisions. But it took a while for me to be able to think like that.' At least Witkowski is in the right place to land a part-time job if he finds himself under-employed by the Monarchs again this season. An economics major at Columbia, he has worked on Wall Street and could always find work on London's Stock Exchange. If things go his way, however, and fate is kinder to John Witkowski, it could be his own stock which is on the rise in 1992.

● **John Witkowski (12) comes under pressure from James Howard** during the 22–7 victory against the Knights.

THE TEAM

Marlon Brown.

MARLON BROWN Finishing third in the league with 7.5 sacks, Brown was named second-team linebacker in the All-World League voting. He set a World League record with 5.5 sacks in the Week Eight game against New York-New Jersey. A former college player at Memphis State and 1989 draft pick of the NFL's Cleveland Browns, his nickname is 'Space Dog', although few people know why. When a female reporter asked Brown why his team-mates called him that, he snarled, 'Because I tell them to.'

DAVID CALDWELL A reserve nose tackle, Caldwell was originally drafted by the San Antonio Riders, but then released. He turned in his best performance in Week Nine against Sacramento, when he made three tackles. Caldwell played at Texas Christian University.

TREVOR CARTHY One of four British players on the Monarchs roster as part of the Operation Discovery programme, Carthy missed much of training camp after suffering a knee injury, but returned to play as a back-up defensive back and on special teams. He previously starred as a running back and cornerback for the Birmingham Bulls in their two Budweiser League triumphs.

DAN CROSSMAN Capping a superb post-season, Crossman was named World Bowl MVP after three interceptions, including one for a touchdown, against Barcelona. In the semi-final against New York-New Jersey, this hard-hitting safety had six tackles. In Week Two, against the same opposition, he blocked a punt and recovered it for a touchdown. Crossman played his college football at Pittsburgh and began the 1991 NFL season on the injured reserve list at the Detroit Lions before being released.

PAT DAVIS One of the best blocking tight ends in the World League, Davis caught his first touchdown pass for the Monarchs in the semi-final victory against New York-New Jersey, giving London the lead for the first time. Drafted by the San Diego Chargers in 1989, he was released by them and then by the Indianapolis Colts. A college player at Syracuse, he took the lead vocals on the Monarchs' rap record, 'Yo Go Monarchs'.

CORRIS ERVIN Named as cornerback on the All World League team, Ervin justified his status as the first defensive back chosen in the World League draft. He added a semi-final interception against New York-New Jersey to his two regular season pick-offs, grabbing a pass deep in Monarchs territory as the Knights drove for a potential match-winning touchdown. After a college career at Central Florida, Ervin was drafted by the NFL's Denver Broncos.

HOWARD FEGGINS A former NFL performer for the New England Patriots, the Monarchs were denied Feggins' skills at cornerback when he missed four weeks with a groin injury. He returned to finish the season strongly, including three tackles in the semi-finals win over New York-New Jersey. A former starter at North Carolina, he was signed but then released by the New York Giants in 1990.

RUSSELL FOSTER A reserve linebacker, Foster proved himself a valuable performer on the special teams. He went to college at Western Kentucky and was chosen by the Monarchs in the supplemental draft. He was the final player cut before the season started, but was brought back to the team in Week Five. Following the World League season, Foster played in the indoor Arena Football League for Orlando as a linebacker and running back.

DAVID HARBOUR A reserve tight end, Harbour played 31 games for the NFL's Washington Redskins in 1988–89. He served as the long snapper on the punt team and came close to winning the same job with the Detroit Lions after the World League season. Harbour attended the University of Illinois and caught one pass for the Monarchs in 1991.

GREG HORNE The sixth-ranked punter in the World League, Horne had an average of 38.7 yards per kick, including a 56-yarder against Sacramento. Following a college career at Arkansas, he was drafted by the NFL's Cincinnati Bengals and played four games for them before signing for the St Louis/Phoenix Cardinals. Horne punted 122 times in the NFL at a 40.6 yards average.

NIGEL HOYTE Another of the Monarchs' home-grown contingent, Londoner Hoyte spent the 1991 season as a reserve defensive lineman and special teams performer. He made four tackles during the regular season and recovered an onside kick against Orlando in Week Three. He experienced American college football when he played for a season at the University of Akron.

MIKE RENNA Recording 6.5 sacks from his defensive end position during the 1991 season, Renna added two more in the semi-final match against New York-New Jersey. A three-year college

starter at Delaware, he signed as a free agent for the Philadelphia Eagles and was then released. Returning to the Eagles after the World League season, Renna played for them at Wembley in the 1991 American Bowl, making a goal-line tackle on Monarchs' team-mate Judd Garrett, who was playing for the Buffalo Bills.

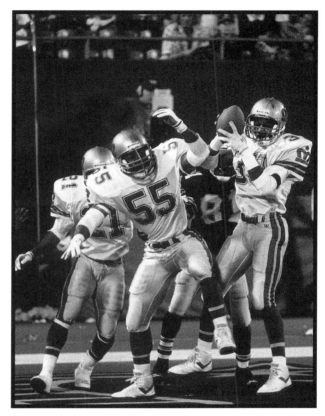

Virgil Robertson (55).

VIRGIL ROBERTSON The first linebacker selected in the World League draft by Frankfurt, Robertson was waived by them and claimed by the Monarchs before the season began. A part-time starter at inside linebacker for the Monarchs, he was a starter at Nicholls State, Louisiana.

KEN SALE A second-team All-World League linebacker, Sale missed out on the Monarchs' World Bowl victory when he injured a hamstring during the semi-final in New York. Released by the San Diego Chargers after a college career at Texas El Paso, he was one of the Monarchs' leading tacklers.

TONY SARGENT A member of the Bomb Squad wide receiving corps, Sargent finished the regular season with 20 catches for 316 yards and four touchdowns. He had two receptions for 24 yards in the semi-final victory over New York-New Jersey. A former college player at Wyoming, Sargent's catches during the regular season were worth 15.8 yards each.

JOHN SHANNON A defensive end, Shannon recorded four sacks and 22 unassisted tackles during the 1991 season. Drafted out of the University of Kentucky by the Chicago Bears, he played in 13 games for the Bears in 1988, as well as making a solo tackle in the play-offs against the San Francisco 49ers. Shannon signed as a free agent for the 49ers in 1990 and again after the World League season, but was cut both times.

JAMES SINGLETARY A linebacker, Singletary went down injured after the fourth week of the season and needed surgery on his left knee. He had to wait until the World Bowl to win back his roster place, when Ken Sale was injured. Singletary was a college player at East Carolina.

CARNEL SMITH A reserve defensive lineman, Smith made two tackles in the Monarchs' semi-final victory and another in the World Bowl against Barcelona. He was drafted by the Indianapolis Colts in 1990 after a college career at Pittsburgh, and was once named *Sports Illustrated*'s Defensive Player of the Week after two sacks against Boston College.

DAVID SMITH Smith scored the first World League touchdown when he rushed for a 28-yard score against Frankfurt. A former Western Kentucky running back, he scored six touchdowns in six games in 1991 before suffering a knee injury. Smith returned to score the final touchdown in the Monarchs' semi-final victory in New York. Drafted by the Philadelphia Eagles, he also had a spell at the Dallas Cowboys and played for the Pittsburgh Gladiators in the Arena Football League.

John Shannon.

IRVIN SMITH The Monarchs' second choice in the draft of defensive backs, Smith started every game at left cornerback and finished the season with 22 unassisted tackles, and two interceptions. He also added four post-season tackles. A starter during his senior year at the University of Maryland, Smith came to the World League after being released by the New York Jets.

RICKEY WILLIAMS One of the league's most underrated players, Williams proved his worth during the post-season with seven tackles and two assists from his linebacker position. He recorded four sacks and forced three fumbles during 1991 and was one of the country's top linebackers during his college career at Arkansas.

HARVEY WILSON A safety who played a key role as an extra defensive back against the New York-New Jersey run-and-shoot offense in the semi-finals, Wilson recorded four tackles, two assists and broke up one pass in that game. He averaged four tackles in the final four games of the 1991 season. Wilson was a former draft pick of the Indianapolis Colts and a starter at Southern University.

London Monarchs head coach Larry Kennan grabs the attention of the 'Bomb Squad': Dana Brinson, Andre Riley, Tony Sargent and Jon Horton.

6
DID YOU KNOW?

WORLD LEAGUE TRIVIA

★ THE first player selected by the World League was **Caesar Rentie,** an offensive tackle out of Oklahoma University, who was chosen by the New York-New Jersey Knights in the first round of the draft for offensive linemen.

★ **Steve Gabbard,** an offensive tackle with NFL play-off experience with the Philadelphia Eagles, Gabbard was the first player selected by the London Monarchs. He had previously played at Wembley for the Eagles in the 1989 American Bowl against the Cleveland Browns.

★ Barcelona Dragons wide receiver **Charles Fryar** is the cousin of New England Patriots wide receiver Irving Fryar.

★ San Antonio Riders started three different quarterbacks in the first three weeks of the 1991 season – **Jason Garrett, Lee Saltz** and **Mike Johnson.** Garrett and Saltz both separated a shoulder in the games they started.

★ Birmingham Fire running back **Steven Avery** plays the guitar, bass, drums and piano and earns a living as a musician when he is not playing football.

★ **Todd Hammel,** quarterback for the New York-New Jersey Knights, has a twin brother called Tadd.

★ How does Sacramento Surge linebacker **Pete Najarian** find time to play football? His vast range of hobbies off the field include flying aeroplanes, sculpting, painting, scuba diving, skiing and surfing.

★ The top-rated passer in the World League's first season was Orlando Thunder running back **Eric Mitchel.** His only pass was a 53-yard touchdown toss to Bruce LaSane, giving him a rating of 158.3, the highest possible score according to the Elias Sports Bureau.

★ The brother of Sacramento Surge safety **Tom Gerhart** is Bobby Gerhart, a professional racing driver on America's Winston Cup circuit.

★ **The New York-New Jersey Knights** got used to getting the sack during 1991. They were the first team to allow 10 sacks (against Barcelona in Week 1) and then allowed a professional football record 14 against the London Monarchs in Week 8.

★ Barcelona Dragons defensive end **Bruce Clark** played in the 1984 Pro Bowl while with the NFL's New Orleans Saints.

★ Birmingham Fire cornerback **Tracy Sanders** has three cousins who have played in the NFL.

★ London Monarchs linebacker **Rickey Williams** plays the cello and studies classical music.

★ The most common degree among players who participated in the first World League draft is criminal justice.

★ Birmingham Fire quarterback **Brent Pease,** the first player chosen in the draft for that position, won All-State honours as a wrestler while at the University of Montana.

★ New York-New Jersey Knights running back **Eric Wilkerson** was the first World League player to rush for more than 100 yards, performing the feat in his team's defeat against the London Monarchs at Wembley in Week 2.

★ Birmingham Fire safety **Arthur Hunter** came face to face with former world heavyweight champion Muhammad Ali on a trip to Michigan and took part in an impromptu shadow boxing session with 'The Greatest'.

★ Barcelona Dragons can claim to have the best baseball team among World League clubs. Cornerback **Adrian Jones** was drafted by the Cincinnati Reds, while quarterback **Tony Rice** was selected by the California Angels.

★ London Monarchs linebacker **James Singletary** is the cousin of Reggie Singletary of the NFL's Philadelphia Eagles.

★ **Montreal Machine** recorded the biggest regular season crowd in the first year of the World League when 53,238 turned up to see their opening home game at the Olympic Stadium against the Barcelona Dragons.

★ The most popular book in the World League, according to a survey of all the players who took part in the league draft, is *The Bible*. The most popular film is *The Godfather*.

★ **Jeff Graham** of the New York–New Jersey Knights was the first quarterback to throw for more than 400 yards when he achieved 411 in a 44–0 victory against the Montreal Machine in their Week 4 meeting.

★ The World League originally wanted its teams to wear a range of colours not previously used in professional football. Pressure of time meant that clothing manufacturers Wilson were able to develop only one new colour, the fluorescent lime-green shirts worn by the Orlando Thunder.

★ Barcelona Dragons defensive end **Jerry Reeses** collects tropical fish.

★ **Joe Campbell** must have been relieved when he was drafted by the New York–New Jersey Knights. The linebacker has a suspicion that dictates he must always wear something black on the field. Black is the Knights' main colour.

★ Barcelona Dragons quarterback **Tony Rice** improved his passing while at Notre Dame University after coach Lou Holtz received a letter from a fan suggesting that he practised by throwing darts.

★ New York–New Jersey Knights linebacker **Ron Sancho** received a humanitarian award in 1986 for saving a truck driver's life after his tanker overturned carrying a full load of hydrochloric acid.

★ Orlando Thunder tight end **Dennis Smith** has a brother, Brian, who plays the son of Hoss Cartwright on American TV's *Bonanza: The Next Generation.*

★ The crowd of 40,875 who attended Barcelona's home game against Orlando was the biggest attendance for a sporting event at Montjuic Stadium, scene of this year's Olympic Games athletics events.

★ The World League experienced the Soviet Block in Week 5, when the Raleigh-Durham Skyhawks defensive end **Oleg Sapega,** an Operation Discovery player from the USSR, blocked a Frankfurt Galaxy extra point attempt.

★ Raleigh-Durham Skyhawks wide receiver **Marvin Hargrove** scored a touchdown with his first reception in high school, college and professional football. His first pro catch was a 34-yard touchdown for the Philadelphia Eagles, his only catch in the NFL.

★ Sacramento Surge tight end **Mel Farr** played for the Los Angeles Rams in the NFC Championship game against the San Francisco 49ers in January 1990, which the Rams lost 30–3.

★ Barcelona Dragon's 29–20 victory over Sacramento in Week 6 was the first overtime game in professional football not to be decided by the first score. WLAF rules call for a six-point margin and the Dragons made sure with a field goal and a touchdown.

★ Sacramento Surge tackle **Mark Nua** was an All-South Pacific high school rugby player while growing up in Auckland, New Zealand.

★ The record for the fastest World League touchdown is held by Orlando Thunder cornerback **Erroll Tucker,** who returned the opening kick-off against Raleigh–Durham in Week 9 for six points, entering the end zone with only 16 seconds having elapsed.

★ Four touchdowns were scored in Birmingham's 24–14 Week 9 victory over New York–New Jersey, none by either team's offense. The Fire scored on an interception return, a fumble return and a fake punt, while the Knights replied a touchdown off a fumble return.

★ **Jim Warne,** tackle for the New York–New Jersey Knights, is a native American Indian. His family is of Sioux origin.

★ The longest single-game road trip of 1991 was recorded by Sacramento, who travelled 5,614 miles to Germany and back to play Frankfurt. They showed no sign of jet lag, becoming the only North American team to win on European soil.

★ Barcelona Dragons wide receiver **Gene Taylor** is training to become an air traffic controller.

7
THE MEN TO WATCH

TONY BAKER (*Frankfurt Galaxy, Running Back*):
Quickly establishing himself as one of the league's
most dangerous running backs, Baker finished the
season with 648 yards, five touchdowns and a place
in the All-World League first team. He proved his
versatility against Orlando in Week 7, catching seven
passes for 173 yards, and earned the nickname of
'The Touchdown Maker'. Baker has NFL experience
with the Atlanta Falcons, the Cleveland Browns and
the Phoenix Cardinals.

JIM BELL (*Barcelona Dragons, Running Back*): A
former draft pick of the San Francisco 49ers, Bell was
a real workhorse in the Barcelona backfield, leading
the team with 367 yards on 137 carries. His highlight
of the season was a 130-yard performance against
Sacramento, catching six passes in the same game.

KENNY BELL (*Birmingham Fire, Running Back*):
A constant threat to opponents, Bell slid out of the
backfield to record a team-leading 40 pass receptions
for 347 yards. He made a name for himself in the
NFL as a kick returner for the Denver Broncos, who
named him their most valuable special teams player
two years running.

KERWIN BELL (*Orlando Thunder, Quarterback*):
Bell took the World League by storm in the opening
two weeks of the season, throwing a total of nine
touchdown passes and winning a pair of Player of
the Week awards. He finished as the league's fourth-
highest rated passer; he also finished his college
career at the University of Florida with the most yards
in Southeastern Conference history.

RICKY BLAKE (*San Antonio Riders, Running
Back*): Blake's runaway train style of running has

earned him the nickname 'Am-Trak', and he finished
third in the league in rushing with 554 yards. He
averaged 4.6 yards per carry and won selection to the
All-World League team before being signed by the
NFL's Dallas Cowboys. Blake proceeded to score a
touchdown against the Cincinnati Bengals on his first
NFL carry.

WILLIE BOUYER (*Birmingham Fire, Wide
Receiver*): Bouyer's 28 catches in 1991 were worth
16.1 yards each and he proved himself a deep threat
with an 87-yard touchdown against Orlando. He gave
a valiant performance in the play-off defeat against
Barcelona, catching nine passes for 115 yards.

JOHN BRANTLEY (*Birmingham Fire, Linebacker*)
Brantley was voted co-Defensive MVP after a 1991
season in which he made 47 tackles – 40 of them solo
– and recorded four sacks. 'Rambo' was good enough
to play nine games for the Houston Oilers in 1989 and
spend three years as a college starter at Georgia,
where he averaged 12 tackles per game.

TIM BROADY (*Frankfurt Galaxy, Safety*): Voted
onto the All-World League second team, despite
being only a seventh round selection in the league's
draft of defensive backs, Broady intercepted two
passes and recorded three and a half sacks. He was
released by the NFL's Seattle Seahawks before
the 1989 season.

BRUCE CLARK (*Barcelona Dragons, Defensive
End*): One of the most experienced players in the
World League, Clark spent seven seasons in the NFL
with the New Orleans Saints and a year with the
Kansas City Chiefs. He led the Dragons with seven
sacks, winning first-team All-World League honours.
He was the winner of the Lombardi Trophy, awarded
to America's top college lineman, in 1978, while at
Penn State University.

GREG COAUETTE (*Sacramento Surge, Safety*): After a season in which Coauette recorded 50 tackles, three interceptions and four sacks in eight games, he was a first-team All-World League selection. He is renowned for his hard hitting. Coauette was voted defensive player of the year at the University of Southern California in 1987.

DEMETRIUS DAVIS (*Barcelona Dragons, Tight End*): Architect of the London Monarchs' only defeat of the season, Davis caught eight passes for 120 yards and two touchdowns in the Dragons' Wembley victory, for which he earned Player of the Week honours. He used his surprising speed for a 220-pounder to haul in 34 passes for 461 yards during the season. He is nicknamed 'Truck'.

MIKE ELKINS (*Sacramento Surge, Quarterback*): Ranked fifth among quarterbacks in the World League in 1991, Elkins threw 13 touchdown passes. He played for the Surge while on the NFL roster of the Kansas City Chiefs, who chose him in the third round of the 1989 draft. He twice surpassed the 300-yard mark with Sacramento, but was cut by the Chiefs before the 1991 NFL season.

SCOTT ERNEY (*Barcelona Dragons, Quarterback*): A solid, if unspectacular, quarterback, Erney was second in the World League passer ratings. He threw eight touchdowns and only two interceptions during the regular season, but had a nightmare in the World Bowl against the London Monarchs, being intercepted four times before half-time. He is the yardage record holder at Rutgers University.

GARRY FRANK (*Frankfurt Galaxy, Guard*): At 292 lb, Frank was the linchpin of the Galaxy offensive line, winning election to the All-World League team. He was chosen in the seventh round of the 1988 NFL draft by the Denver Broncos and was a first round selection by Frankfurt. Frank was two-time Southeastern Conference shot putt champion while at Mississippi State University.

MONTY GILBREATH (*New York-New Jersey Knights, Wide Receiver*): Gilbreath tied for sixth place in the league with 40 catches. His 643 receiving yards was fifth best, but he was restricted to just one touchdown. He topped the 100-yard mark three times, fulfilling the promise he showed in college at San Diego State.

RON GOETZ (*Barcelona Dragons, Linebacker*): Scourge of opposition running backs and quarterbacks, Goetz made 50 tackles, including 44 unassisted, and grabbed four interceptions. A former draft pick of the Minnesota Vikings, he won All-Big Ten honours at the University of Minnesota.

JEFF GRAHAM (*New York-New Jersey Knights, Quarterback*): Graham overcame 62 sacks to finish third in the league's passer ratings by throwing for 2,407 yards in the Knights' run-and-shoot offense. Despite the hammering he took, Graham never missed a game through injury and averaged 15.3 yards per completion, the best in the league, as well as rushing for six touchdowns.

●Scott Erney (left), was one of the league's most consistent performers last season.

MARVIN HARGROVE (*1991 Raleigh-Durham Skyhawks, Wide Receiver*): Hargrove held at least one pass in every game in 1991, ending up with 38 receptions, ninth best in the league, for 424 yards. In 1990 he walked into the Philadelphia Eagles training camp and asked for a try-out, winning a job as kick returner and scoring a touchdown against the Phoenix Cardinals with his only NFL catch.

ELROY HARRIS (*Birmingham Fire, Running Back*): Although Harris was waived by Montreal during the 1991 season, Birmingham had seen enough of him in their two games against the Machine – during which he rushed for 194 yards – to sign him. He gained 290 yards in six games during the Fire's play-off push, finishing as the league's fourth leading rusher with 540 yards.

CLARKSTON HINES (*1991 Raleigh-Durham Skyhawks, Wide Receiver*): A big-play threat, Hines gained 614 yards on 31 catches, an average of 19.8 yards per reception. He set an NCAA record during his college career at Duke, catching 38 touchdown passes and topping 1,000 receiving yards for a season on three occasions.

JOHN HOLLAND (*Birmingham Fire, Cornerback*): Holland's 38 tackles and three interceptions won him a place on the All-World League second team and helped turn the Fire secondary into one of the most formidable units in the league. His only previous professional experience was a season with the Canadian League's British Columbia Lions.

JASON JOHNSON (*Frankfurt Galaxy, Wide Receiver*): Johnson gained NFL experience as a kick returner for the Denver Broncos and Pittsburgh Steelers, before gaining 635 yards on 38 catches for the Galaxy. The highlight of his season was a 54-yard reception to set up Frankfurt's last-gasp win against Raleigh-Durham.

BOBBY McALLISTER (*1991 Raleigh-Durham Skyhawks, Quarterback*): One of the most athletic quarterbacks in the league, McAllister proved his ability as a passer by throwing for 502 yards and five touchdowns in two games against Orlando. He enjoyed an outstanding college career at Michigan State, and led them to the Rose Bowl and Gator Bowl in his final two years at school.

PAT McGUIRK (*1991 Raleigh-Durham Skyhawks, Cornerback*): McGuirk's six interceptions were third best in the league. He enjoyed a big day against the London Monarchs, recovering two fumbles and intercepting a pass. An All-Golden State Conference selection while at the College of San Mateo, he was released in 1990 by the Winnipeg Blue Bombers of the Canadian Football League.

JOHN MILLER (*Birmingham Fire, Safety*): A key member of the Fire secondary which combined for 21 interceptions, Miller recorded six himself and won a place in the All-World League team. He holds the league record with 99-yard interception return for a touchdown against Sacramento. He played for the NFL's Detroit Lions in 1989 and 1990 and was a college star at Michigan State.

ERIC MITCHEL (*Orlando Thunder, Running Back*): Averaging 6.7 yards per rushing attempt and holding 26 passes, Mitchel proved himself one of the league's best all-purpose backs and earned second-team All-World League honours. He scored three rushing touchdowns against Sacramento and returned a kick-off 96 yards for a touchdown against Montreal.

CHRIS MOHR (*Montreal Machine, Punter*): Chosen in the sixth round of the 1989 NFL draft by Tampa Bay Buccaneers, Mohr proceeded to earn selection to the league's All-Rookie team. He even managed to score an extra point against the Chicago Bears by running into the end zone with a fumbled snap. He was a first-team All-World Leaguer after averaging 42.7 yards per punt in 1991.

MARK MRAZ (*Frankfurt Galaxy, Defensive End*): Mraz played for Atlanta Falcons and the Los Angeles Raiders in the NFL before being a second-round draft selection by the Galaxy. He recorded six and a half sacks and was voted onto the All-World League team. He enjoyed successful college career at Utah State.

PETE NAJARIAN (*Sacramento Surge, Linebacker*): A well travelled linebacker, Najarian played for the Minnesota Vikings, the Tampa Bay Buccaneers and Canada's Toronto Argonauts before finding a home at Sacramento. A physical player, he proved his toughness by playing two games with a broken thumb before undergoing surgery. He won second-team All-World League honours.

FALANDA NEWTON (*New York-New Jersey Knights, Safety*): Newton was the unlikeliest success story of the season after being the penultimate player chosen in the last round of the draft for defensive backs. He proceeded to intercept eight passes, the second best in the league, and set a WLAF record with three in one game against London. He led the Knights with 73 tackles.

BJORN NITTMO (*Montreal Machine, Kicker*): Nittmo set a league record by landing a 50-yard field goal against San Antonio, one of 13 successes out of 18 attempts during the season – a record which made him a second team All-World League selection. He scored 39 points in six games for the NFL's New York Giants in 1989 and played in the 1991 American Bowl at Wembley for Buffalo.

CARL PAINTER (*Orlando Thunder, Running Back*): Painter was the top kick-off returner in the league with a 24.9 average, including his league-record six returns for 178 yards against New York-New Jersey. He played in the NFL for two seasons with the Detroit Lions.

PAUL PALMER (*Barcelona Dragons, Running Back*): One of the biggest names to be signed by the WLAF, Palmer was a first-round draft choice of the NFL's Kansas City Chiefs in 1987. He also played for the Dallas Cowboys and the Detroit Lions. He gained 319 yards in the first four weeks of the 1991 season, but a hamstring injury restricted him to only 39 yards for the rest of the year.

ANTHONY PARKER (*New York-New Jersey Knights, Cornerback*): Parker intimidated quarterbacks with his ability to pick off passes, leading the league with 11 interceptions and sharing the WLAF's Defensive MVP Award. He scored two touchdowns and only twice finished games without an interception. He was the only unanimous choice on the All-World League defense.

CARL PARKER (*Sacramento Surge, Wide Receiver*): Parker ranked third in the league in both receptions, with 52, and yardage, with 801 yards. He tied for second place with eight touchdown catches. A former Cincinnati Bengals player, Parker caught touchdown passes in the last seven games of the 1991 season and topped 100 yards on three occasions.

MIKE PEREZ (*Frankfurt Galaxy, Quarterback*): Perez threw for 2,272 yards and 13 touchdowns during the season, leading Frankfurt to the league's third-best record. A graduate of San Jose State, Perez was drafted by the New York Giants in 1988 and came close to beating Jeff Hostetler, an eventual Super Bowl hero, for a place on the Giants roster.

MICHAEL PROCTOR (*Montreal Machine, Quarterback*): A fine rushing quarterback, Proctor gained 247 yards on just 41 carries, scoring two touchdowns. He added 1,222 yards and three touchdowns when throwing the ball. Released by the NFL's New England Patriots in 1990, Proctor threw for 8,210 yards in his college career at Murray State.

TONY RICE (*Barcelona Dragons, Quarterback*): A former cover star of *Sports Illustrated* during an illustrious college career, Rice led an unbeaten Notre Dame team to the National Championship in 1988. He had a 28-3 record as a starter at Notre Dame, but started only three games for Barcelona. An elusive runner, he averaged 6.4 yards per carry and scored two touchdowns in 1991.

RON SANCHO (*New York-New Jersey Knights, Linebacker*): Sancho scored three touchdowns from his linebacker position, including blocking a punt and recovering it in the end zone against Montreal. A former draft pick of the NFL's Kansas City Chiefs, he added six sacks to his 69 tackles and was named to the All-World League second team.

RICHARD SHELTON (*Montreal Machine, Cornerback*): Shelton was World League Player of the Week after scoring touchdowns on a 25-yard fumble return and a 63-yard interception against Birmingham. He scored twice in one match again when he returned a kick-off 90 yards and a punt 67 against Sacramento, performances which earned him second-team All-World League honours. He is a former NFL player with the Denver Broncos and the Pittsburgh Steelers, whom he rejoined in 1991.

TRACY SIMIEN (*Montreal Machine, Linebacker*): Simien earned selection to the All-World League first team by recording 33 tackles and five sacks. He played in an NFL play-off game for the Denver Broncos and appeared for the Kansas City Chiefs during the 1991 NFL season. Simien spent the previous season on the Chiefs' practice roster.

GENE TAYLOR (*Barcelona Dragons, Wide Receiver*): Among the league leaders in all categories for his position, Taylor finished second in yards per catch with 21.3, fourth in yardage with 745 and fourth in touchdowns with six. A former NFL player with the Tampa Bay Buccaneers, he enjoyed his best game of the 1991 season against Orlando, catching five passes for 163 yards and two touchdowns.

MIKE TEETER (*Frankfurt Galaxy, Nose Tackle*): Teeter anchored the league's top-ranked defense from his position in the centre of the defensive line, where he was often double-teamed by opponents. Named to the All-World League first team after finishing the season with three sacks, he played in three Rose Bowls while at college at Michigan.

ERROLL TUCKER (*Orlando Thunder, Cornerback*): Tucker was voted the top special teams player in the league after averaging a WLAF-best 20.7 yards on 18 punt returns. His seven kick-off returns were worth an impressive 37 yards each. He is a former return man for the NFL's Buffalo Bills and the New England Patriots.

LONNIE TURNER (*New York-New Jersey Knights, Wide Receiver*): An experienced player, Turner

appeared for three different teams in the now-defunct USFL before finishing the World League season with 41 pass receptions, fifth best in the league, for 629 yards. He twice went above 100 yards receiving in a game, gaining 146 yards against Montreal and 122 against London at Wembley.

TIM WALTON (*San Antonio Riders, Linebacker*): Walton led the Riders with 50 tackles and seven sacks thanks to an aggressive style of play. He forced three fumbles and recovered three, while deflecting 14 passes. He was released by the NFL's Detroit Lions in 1989. Walton was named Ball State's MVP as a college senior in 1988.

ERIC WILKERSON (*New York-New Jersey Knights, Running Back*): Wilkerson led the league in rushing with 717 yards and tied for the league lead with 11 touchdowns to earn second-team All-World League honours. He scored three times against Orlando and set a WLAF record with a 74-yard rush against the London Monarchs. Wilkerson proved his versatility with 26 catches for the Knights. He was on the Pittsburgh Steelers' active roster for the 1990 NFL play-offs.

BYRON WILLIAMS (*Orlando Thunder, Wide Receiver*): Joint top touchdown scorer in the league with 11, Williams scored three touchdowns in the opening game victory against San Antonio. Four 100-yard receiving games helped make up his season total of 811 yards on 59 catches, second best in the league. He caught 59 passes in three seasons with the NFL's New York Giants.

New York-New Jersey Knights safety Falanda Newton brings down London Monarchs receiver Dana Brinson. Newton, a 12th-round draft choice, was one of the surprise stars of the 1991 season.

8
CONQUERING EUROPE

THEY loved it in London, went barmy in Barcelona and frantic in Frankfurt. All over Europe the World League's arrival last year was greeted with a fervour usually reserved for visits by American rock stars like Madonna, Prince and Bruce Springsteen.

When the NFL announced the formation of the World League and stressed its aim of 'globalising' the sport there were a few raised eyebrows. It was one thing encouraging people to switch on their televisions once a week to watch skilfully packaged, colourful programmes featuring NFL highlights. It was a completely different ball game to get the same people to leave the comfort of their homes and spend their cash to watch teams consisting of largely unknown players in a supposedly inferior league.

League officials conservatively set their sights on average crowds of 15,000 for the European Division. Somewhere they must have got their sums wrong. By the end of the season, the London Monarchs had averaged more than 40,000 fans per game, while the Barcelona Dragons and the Frankfurt Galaxy each fell a few hundred short of the 30,000 mark, proving that even a language barrier could not halt the league's progress. Already, Paris is being hotly tipped to be awarded a team when the competition expands to 12 teams for the 1993 season.

It wasn't just the size of the crowds that was so encouraging for the future of the World League. What was more impressive was the manner in which the fans adopted their teams, turned those unknown players into stars, and lived and died on the fortunes of their club. In Barcelona, potentially the most difficult of the European markets to crack, thousands of fans waited at the airport to greet the Dragons on their return from a two-game trip to the U.S. and many more lined the street leading to the team's headquarters. Dragons coach Jack Bicknell became a celebrity with his larger-than-life personality and was christened '*El Cabalero*' – the Cowboy. 'It's sort of

funny when people recognise you in a foreign country,' admits Bicknell, who highlights another reason for believing that the World League's future in Europe is a bright one. 'A lot of young people came to the games, it was a very young crowd. A lot of the older people in Barcelona are entrenched in soccer and that's understandable. But the younger ones wanted to see the spectacle of American football and it really took off.'

In Frankfurt, where the final game of the season was a sell-out of almost 52,000, Galaxy general manager Oliver Luck expects even bigger things this year. 'We're starting up much further down the road than last season,' he says. 'Last year we sold only 450 season tickets. This year it could be 50 times that.'

Much of the groundwork for the league's European success was laid by Monarchs general manager Billy

Hicks in his previous position as European co-ordinator. 'I think it is the right game at the right time,' says Hicks when asked to explain why Europe proved such a success story while the six teams in the U.S. could produce an average crowd of only just over 20,000. 'We have provided everything we said we were going to provide. The product is there, not only exciting football but also the method of sports and spectacle presentation that is surprising and new to the Europeans.'

What also helped, of course, was that the European Division boasted the three best teams in the league, with the Monarchs finishing the regular season with a 9–1 record, Barcelona 8–2 and Frankfurt 7–3. 'Word of mouth spreads and the success of these three teams has had something to do with it, but I don't think you can say the league did well over here just because the teams were winning their matches. There is much more to the mix than that,' Hicks argues.

Having helped start the ball rolling and spent hours convincing people of the World League's viability in Europe, Hicks took great pride in the league's achievements on this side of the Atlantic last spring. 'There were times during the two years leading up to the league starting when I had doubts. I came up against continual cynicism and constant road blocks. When you don't have the team or the fireworks to show to people in the meeting room it can get frustrating, but I always felt we could make something happen in Europe.' And while TV viewers in the U.S. were slow to catch the bout of World League fever which afflicted London, Barcelona and Frankfurt, Hicks is convinced that the league's European influence will help the U.S. to catch the bug. 'I think much of the romance of this league to Americans is the international presence. You can be sitting with a bag of chips and a beer on your couch in Des Moines, Iowa, and suddenly it's over to ABC live from the Montjuic Stadium, Barcelona, and they are showing a shot you've never seen before. There is a great appeal to that.'

The London Monarchs, pictured here with commentator Cincinnati Bengals quarterback Boomer Esiason (back row, centre).

9

THE
WEMBLEY EXPERIENCE

FOR those British sports fans brought up on the non-caring attitude of a large number of the nation's top soccer clubs, a trip to Wembley Stadium for a London Monarchs home game is an enlightening experience. At far too many grounds, the soccer fan is made to feel like a second-class citizen by teams who smugly believe he will continue to turn up every week, come what may, and that a few pop records are sufficient to keep him entertained before the game and during half-time. The Monarchs, however, have shown that a different method of presentation does exist. A World League game at Wembley is a potent mix of sport, circus, rock concert and Cockney knees-up. Far from leaving the fans who turn up 90 minutes before kick-off with nothing to do but read their programme, the Monarchs lay on a menu of marching bands, cartoon characters, jugglers, magicians and even giant inflatable Sumo wrestlers. And, of course, no sporting event with its roots in the U.S. would be complete without cheerleaders, and even in these enlightened days of sexual equality The Crown Jewels can be guaranteed a welcome almost as frenzied as that of the Monarchs themselves. That is not to say that the Wembley crowd is dominated by beer-swilling males in the same way as soccer. A Monarchs audience is a refreshing mix of sex, social class and age – although the young outnumber the old, providing promise of a whole generation growing up as Monarchs fans.

Once the game begins, there is no danger of the fans being left to their own devices during the breaks in play. Every spare moment is filled with snatches of rock music carefully chosen to complement the action. Several times during each game, the old stadium will reverberate to the pounding beat of Queen's 'We Will Rock You', while each Monarchs touchdown is greeted with a chorus of 'All Right

Now'. The highlight for the fan with happy feet comes during the change of ends after the third quarter, when the whole crowd is invited to stand up and boogie to Aretha Franklin's 'Respect'. And they do – even in the Royal Box. Throw in the half-time fireworks display, the odd jazz band and a giant screen showing action replays and you have a sports and entertainment coalition that left the Monarchs averaging 40,000 fans per game last season.

'There is a lot of competition for the entertainment dollar these days,' says Monarchs general manager Billy Hicks. 'The biggest thing for us to accomplish was to let people know that the London Monarchs represent American football at the top level, plus family fun, the American spectacle and razzmatazz.'

If the fans quickly fell in love with the Monarchs, then the players equally swiftly became intoxicated by the Wembley atmosphere. 'Honest to God, there is nowhere in this league I would rather be playing than in London,' says Monarchs wide receiver and fan favourite Jon Horton. 'The crowd gets behind you 100 per cent no matter what you do.'

Dana Brinson was another who immediately warmed to his surroundings. 'I love Wembley – the stadium, the playing field, the crowd, everything. I really appreciated the way they took me. It really makes you respond. And they surprised us with how much they know about the sport. They know exactly when they ought to cheer and when they should boo, which I didn't expect.'

Coach Larry Kennan spent nine years in the National Football League, one of America's biggest and most successful entertainment machines, but feels the Wembley spectacle is a match for anything the NFL can offer. 'This is big-time right here,' he says. 'There is a big-time atmosphere with all the pre game and half-time shows. This organisation is doing an excellent job and we put on a heck of a show – tha goes for the office staff, the players and the fans.'

Hicks insists that the glitter surrounding the Monarchs games is not intended to dazzle the fans into failing to notice that World League football is inferior to the more familiar NFL. 'This has become a nation of football experts,' he says. 'They know they are watching a good product.'

But even if the Wembley crowd is as knowledgeable as an American one, the thing the players love is that they don't yet have the Stateside fans' more cynical approach to the game. Hardly a single spectator leaves a Monarchs game until the final bar of 'Land of Hope and Glory' has risen into the evening sky at the end of the match. 'They are more like an American college crowd here,' says quarterback Stan Gelbaugh. 'It's amazing that no one leaves, even when the game is out of reach. In the States the place would be empty, but here they never lose interest.' Well of course they don't. Queen, Aretha, Popeye, Betty Boop and a couple of inflatable Sumo wrestlers see to that.

Roy Hart (left), Mike enna (95) and Dedrick dge (33) lead the ndon Monarchs' grand trance at Wembley.

Right: The Wembley fans revelled in the party atmosphere surrounding London Monarchs matches and quickly took their new team to their hearts.

10
WORLD LEAGUE RECORDS

SCORING

● MOST POINTS 18
Jeff Alexander, LONDON at
Sacramento 18.5.91
Eric Mitchel, ORLANDO *v.*
Sacramento, 11.5.91
Eric Wilkerson, NY/NJ *v.* Orlando,
27.4.91
Jon Horton, LONDON *v.* Montreal,
20.4.91
Byron Williams, ORLANDO *v.* San
Antonio, 25.3.91

● MOST TOUCHDOWNS 3
Jeff Alexander, LONDON at
Sacramento, 18.5.91
Eric Mitchel, ORLANDO *v.*
Sacramento, 11.5.91
Eric Wilkerson, NY/NJ *v.* Orlando,
27.4.91
Jon Horton, LONDON *v.* Montreal,
20.4.91
Byron Williams, ORLANDO *v.* San
Antonio, 25.3.91

● MOST FIELD GOALS 4
Bjorn Nittmo, MONTREAL *v.*
Orlando, 27.5.91

**● MOST FIELD GOAL
ATTEMPTS 5**
Massimo Manca, BARCELONA *v.*
Birmingham, 4.5.91
John Nies, SACRAMENTO *v.*
Montreal, 4.5.91

**● LONGEST FIELD
GOAL 50 yards**
Bjorn Nittmo, MONTREAL at San
Antonio, 19.5.91

**● LONGEST FIELD GOAL
ATTEMPT 54 yards**
Teddy Garcia, SAN ANTONIO *v.*
Frankfurt, 1.4.91

**● MOST POINTS AFTER
TOUCHDOWN 7**
Charlie Baumann, ORLANDO *v.*
Raleigh-Durham, 30.3.91

RUSHING

● MOST YARDS 140
Ricky Blake, SAN ANTONIO at
Raleigh-Durham, 15.4.91

● MOST CARRIES 31
Jim Bell, BARCELONA at
Sacramento, 27.4.91

● MOST TOUCHDOWNS 3
Jeff Alexander, LONDON at
Sacramento, 18.5.91
Eric Mitchel, ORLANDO *v.*
Sacramento, 11.5.91
Eric Wilkerson, NY/NJ *v.* Orlando,
27.4.91

**● LONGEST RUNS
74 yards**
Eric Wilkerson, NY/NJ at London,
31.3.91

PASSING

● MOST YARDS 411
Jeff Graham, NY/NJ at Montreal,
13.4.91.

● MOST ATTEMPTS 48
Mike Perez, FRANKFURT at
Sacramento, 13.4.91

**● MOST COMPLETIONS
29**
Stan Gelbaugh, LONDON *v.* Raleigh-
Durham, 28.4.91
Kerwin Bell, ORLANDO *v.* Raleigh-
Durham, 30.3.91

**● LONGEST COMPLETION
6 yards**
Stan Gelbaugh to Jon Horton,
LONDON at Frankfurt 23.3.91

**● MOST TOUCHDOWN
PASSES 5**
Kerwin Bell, ORLANDO *v.* San
Antonio, 25.3.91

**● MOST ATTEMPTS
WITHOUT
INTERCEPTION 44**
Kerwin Bell, ORLANDO *v.* Raleigh-
Durham, 30.3.91

**● INTERCEPTIONS
THROWN 18**
Mike Perez, FRANKFURT *v.*
Sacramento, 25.5.91
Eric Jones, BIRMINGHAM at
Barcelona, 4.5.91
Mike Elkins, SACRAMENTO *v.*
Barcelona, 27.4.91
Kerwin Bell, ORLANDO *v.*
Birmingham, 21.4.91
Kerwin Bell, ORLANDO at London,
6.4.91
Brent Pease, BIRMINGHAM at
Montreal, 8.4.91

RECEIVING

● MOST YARDS 196
Jon Horton, LONDON at Sacramento,
18.5.91

● MOST RECEPTIONS 12
Judd Garrett, LONDON at
Birmingham, 15.4.91

● MOST TOUCHDOWNS 3
Jon Horton, LONDON *v.* Montreal,
20.4.91
Byron Williams, ORLANDO *v.* San
Antonio, 25.3.91

**● LONGEST RECEPTION
96 yards**
Jon Horton, LONDON at Frankfurt,
23.3.91

PUNTING

● MOST YARDS 407
Chris Mohr, MONTREAL at London,
20.4.91

● MOST PUNTS 10
Chris Mohr, MONTREAL at London,
20.4.91

● FEWEST PUNTS 1
Greg Horne, LONDON *v.* Raleigh-
Durham, 28.4.91
Bob Lilljedahl, NY/NJ *v.* Sacramento,
22.4.91

**● LONGEST PUNT
80 yards**
Luis Aguiar, BARCELONA at
Sacramento, 27.4.91

**● MOST PUNTS INSIDE
OPPONENTS' 20 4**
Kirk Maggio, BIRMINGHAM at
Frankfurt, 11.5.91

PUNT RETURNS

● MOST YARDS 114
Erroll Tucker, ORLANDO at NY/NJ,
27.4.91

● MOST RETURNS 8
Elliott Searcy, SAN ANTONIO *v.*
Birmingham, 29.4.91

**● LONGEST RETURN
73 yds**
James Henry, BIRMINGHAM at
Frankfurt, 12.5.91

KICK-OFF RETURNS

● MOST YARDS 178
Carl Painter, ORLANDO at NY/NJ
27.4.91

● MOST RETURNS 6
Carl Painter, ORLANDO at NY/NJ,
27.4.91

**● LONGEST RETURN
96 yds**
Eric Mitchel, ORLANDO at Montreal
27.5.91

INTERCEPTIONS

**● MOST INTERCEPTIONS
3**
Falanda Newton, NY/NJ *v.* London,
11.5.91

● MOST YARDS 99
John Miller, BIRMINGHAM *v.*
Sacramento, 30.3.91

● LONGEST RETURN 99
John Miller, BIRMINGHAM *v.*
Sacramento, 30.3.91

SACKS

● MOST SACKS 5.5
Marlon Brown, LONDON at NY/NJ,
11.5.91

SINGLE GAME TEAM RECORDS

SCORING

● MOST POINTS 58
ORLANDO v. Raleigh-Durham, 30.3.91

● FEWEST POINTS 0
MONTREAL v. NY/NJ, 13.4.91
BIRMINGHAM v. London, 15.4.91

● MOST POINTS, BOTH TEAMS 78
Orlando 58, Raleigh-Durham 20, 30.3.91

● FEWEST POINTS, BOTH TEAMS 12
Sacramento 9, Raleigh-Durham 3, 23.3.91

● MOST TOUCHDOWNS 7
ORLANDO v. Raleigh-Durham, 30.3.91

● MOST TOUCHDOWNS, BOTH TEAMS 11
Orlando (6) v. Sacramento (5), 11.5.91

● MOST POINTS 1ST QUARTER 14
FRANKFURT at NY/NJ, 6.4.91
LONDON at Sacramento, 18.5.91
ORLANDO v. San Antonio, 25.3.91
ORLANDO v. Sacramento, 11.5.91
SACRAMENTO at NY/NJ, 22.4.91

● MOST POINTS 2ND QUARTER 21
BARCELONA at Montreal, 1.4.91
LONDON at San Antonio, 6.5.91
NY/NJ v. Orlando, 27.4.91
NY/NJ v. San Antonio, 25.5.91

● MOST POINTS 3RD QUARTER 19
LONDON v. NY/NJ, 31.3.91

● MOST POINTS 4TH QUARTER 20
ORLANDO at Montreal, 27.5.91

● MOST POINTS, BOTH TEAMS, 1ST QUARTER 21
Orlando (14) v. San Antonio (7), 25.3.91
Orlando (14) v. Sacramento (7), 11.5.91
Sacramento (14) at NY/NJ (7), 22.4.91

● MOST POINTS, BOTH TEAMS, 2ND QUARTER 24
Orlando (17) v. Raleigh-Durham (7), 30.3.91
London (17) at Sacramento (7), 18.5.91

● MOST POINTS, BOTH TEAMS, 3RD QUARTER 23
Barcelona (16) v. Orlando (7), 14.4.91

● MOST POINTS, BOTH TEAMS, 4TH QUARTER 38
Orlando (20) at Montreal (18), 27.5.91

● MOST POINTS AFTER TOUCHDOWN 7
ORLANDO v. Raleigh-Durham, 30.3.91

● MOST POINTS AFTER TOUCHDOWN, BOTH TEAMS 9
London (6) at Sacramento (3), 18.5.91
Orlando (7) v. Raleigh-Durham (2), 30.3.91
Orlando (6) v. Sacramento (3), 11.5.91

● MOST FIELD GOALS 4
MONTREAL v. Orlando, 27.5.91

● MOST FIELD GOALS, BOTH TEAMS 5
Barcelona (3) at Sacramento (2), 27.4.91
Sacramento (3) at Montreal (2), 4.5.91

FIRST DOWNS

● MOST FIRST DOWNS 29
ORLANDO v. Raleigh-Durham, 30.3.91

● FEWEST FIRST DOWNS 6
BIRMINGHAM v. San Antonio, 29.4.91

● MOST FIRST DOWNS, BOTH TEAMS 47
Sacramento (27) at Orlando (20), 11.5.91

● FEWEST FIRST DOWNS, BOTH TEAMS 18
Birmingham (6) v. San Antonio (12), 29.4.91

● MOST FIRST DOWNS RUSHING 19
BARCELONA at Sacramento, 27.4.91

● FEWEST FIRST DOWNS RUSHING 0
SAN ANTONIO at NY/NJ, 25.5.91

● MOST FIRST DOWNS PASSING 22
ORLANDO v. Raleigh-Durham, 30.3.91

● FEWEST FIRST DOWNS PASSING 2
BIRMINGHAM v. San Antonio, 29.4.91
MONTREAL at Birmingham, 23.3.91
MONTREAL v. Birmingham, 8.4.91

● MOST FIRST DOWNS BY PENALTY 5
MONTREAL v. NY/NJ, 13.4.91

NET YARDS GAINED

● MOST NET YARDS 506
ORLANDO v. Raleigh-Durham, 30.3.91

● FEWEST NET YARDS 90
BIRMINGHAM at Frankfurt, 12.5.91.

● MOST NET YARDS, BOTH TEAMS 815
Orlando (506) v. Raleigh-Durham (309), 30.3.91

● FEWEST NET YARDS, BOTH TEAMS 375
Birmingham (128) v. San Antonio (231), 23.3.91

RUSHING

● MOST ATTEMPTS 52
BARCELONA at Sacramento, 27.4.91

● FEWEST ATTEMPTS 11
BIRMINGHAM at Barcelona, 4.5.91
LONDON v. Barcelona, 27.5.91

● MOST YARDS GAINED 290
SAN ANTONIO at Raleigh-Durham, 15.4.91

● FEWEST YARDS GAINED 14
BIRMINGHAM at Frankfurt, 12.5.91

PASSING

● MOST ATTEMPTS 54
ORLANDO v. Raleigh-Durham, 30.3.91

● FEWEST ATTEMPTS 12
BIRMINGHAM v. San Antonio, 29.4.91

● MOST PASSES COMPLETED 35
ORLANDO v. Raleigh-Durham, 30.3.91

● FEWEST PASSES COMPLETED 4
BIRMINGHAM v. San Antonio, 29.4.91

● MOST YARDS GAINED 504
NY/NJ at Montreal, 13.4.91

● FEWEST YARDS GAINED 29
NY/NJ v. Frankfurt, 6.4.91

● MOST TIMES SACKED 14
NY/NJ v. London, 11.5.91

INTERCEPTIONS

● MOST INTERCEPTIONS BY 4
BARCELONA v. Birmingham, 5.4.91
BARCELONA at Sacramento, 27.4.91
BIRMINGHAM at Orlando, 21.4.91
BIRMINGHAM at Raleigh-Durham, 25.5.91
BIRMINGHAM v. San Antonio, 29.4.91
LONDON v. Orlando, 6.4.91
MONTREAL v. Birmingham, 8.4.91
NY/NJ at Raleigh-Durham, 5.5.91
SACRAMENTO at Frankfurt, 25.5.91

● MOST INTERCEPTIONS, BOTH TEAMS 7
Birmingham (4) at Raleigh-Durham (3), 25.5.91

● MOST YARDS 102
BIRMINGHAM at Orlando, 21.4.91

● MOST TOUCHDOWNS 2
NY/NJ v. Frankfurt, 6.4.91

PUNT RETURNS

● MOST RETURNS 8
SAN ANTONIO v. Birmingham, 29.4.91

● MOST YARDS 114
ORLANDO at NY/NJ, 27.4.91

KICK-OFF RETURNS

● MOST RETURNS 9
RALEIGH-DURHAM at Orlando, 30.3.91

● MOST YARDS 249
ORLANDO at Montreal, 27.5.91

PENALTIES

● MOST PENALTIES 15
LONDON at NY/NJ, 11.5.91

● FEWEST PENALTIES 1
ORLANDO v. Birmingham, 21.4.91

● MOST YARDS 125
FRANKFURT at NY/NJ, 6.4.91

● FEWEST YARDS 10
BARCELONA at London, 27.5.91

● Jeff Alexander dives over the line to score in San Antonio.

11
THE BASICS OF AMERICAN FOOTBALL

NO matter how complicated the action may appear to viewers discovering American football for the first time through ITV's coverage of the World League, the aims of the game are relatively straightforward. Each team is attempting to move the ball into the area behind their opponent's goal line (the *end zone*) for a touchdown, or to get near enough to kick the ball through the posts at the end of the field. Here's how they do it.

Progress in American football is measured in yards. Any time a team has the ball – known as being *'on offense'* – it has four chances, or *downs*, to gain 10 yards. If a team achieves that distance or more it keeps the ball and is allowed to start a fresh set of four downs, which is called *making a first down*. For example, if the team gains three yards on its first play they start their second down needing another seven yards. This is called *second and seven*. If they then made three more, it would be *third and four*.

If a team uses its four downs and fails to make 10 yards, the opponents take over possession at the point where the last play broke down. If a team has failed to gain its 10 yards on the first three plays it will usually use the fourth down to punt the ball deep into the opponent's territory to avoid handing over possession in a dangerous position on the field.

There are several ways to score points:

Touchdown (6 points) To score a touchdown, a runner has to break the vertical plane of the goal line with the ball, with the ball in his possession. A touchdown can also be scored by a player standing in the end zone and catching a pass, or recovering a fumbled ball.

Conversion (1 point) Also called an *extra point*, it is like a conversion in rugby. The kicker has to put the ball between the uprights.

Two point conversion Unlike the NFL, teams in the World League can try for two extra points after a touchdown by running or passing the ball into the end zone.

Field goal (3 points) If a team is near the opponent's end zone but has failed to make 10 yards with its first three downs, it may try to score a field goal on fourth down. Again, the ball has to be kicked through the uprights.

Safety (2 points) This is scored when a defensive player tackles the ball carrier behind his goal line. The field is 100 yards in length, plus 10 yards either end for the end zones and there are two basic methods of advancing downfield with the ball:

Running The quarterback, after receiving the ball from the centre, will turn and hand it to one of his running backs, (this is known as a *hand-off*), who runs downfield until he is tackled, signalling the end of the play.

Passing The quarterback, instead of handing off, throws the ball forward to one of his players, who, after catching it, is free to run with the ball until tackled. Only one forward pass is allowed per down and it must be made from behind the point where the play started (the *line of scrimmage*). If the pass misses the receiver and hits the ground it is ruled an *incomplete pass*, the ball is dead and the next down starts from the same place as the last one. If a defender catches the pass his team takes over possession from the point where the defender was tackled with the ball.

What confuses most new watchers of American football is the large number of extremely large men who appear to be tackling each other with the ball nowhere near them. What is actually going on is *blocking*. The players on the same side as the ball carrier are trying to push their opponents out of the way and clear a path for the man with the ball. Obviously the defensive players are trying to shake them off and make the tackle.

When the quarterback drops back behind the line of scrimmage to pass, the offensive linemen form a wall around him and try to keep the opponents at bay while he finds a man to pass to. Again, those defenders who are not trying to cover the men likely to receive a pass are trying to force their way into *the pocket* to *sack* the quarterback before he throws the ball.

The game is divided into four quarters of 15 minutes each. The first and third quarters begin with a kick-off, the second and fourth continue with the existing sequence of play. The clock stops when the ball goes dead, i.e. the ball carrier goes out of bounds, or the quarterback throws an incomplete pass. Each team can stop the clock three times per half by calling a time-out.

PLAYS TO LOOK FOR

Blitz This is a defensive play designed to increase the pressure on the quarterback. Linebackers and/or defensive backs leave their area of pass coverage and instead try to get to the quarterback before he can throw the ball.

Bomb The most exciting play in football, this is the long pass downfield. The offense will try to isolate one or more receivers against just one defender. In an attempt to attract the attention of the defense away from the deep receiver, the quarterback may use the *pump fake* – pretending to throw to another receiver. When the London Monarchs use the bomb the receiver is usually Jon Horton.

Bootleg In a bootleg the quarterback fakes a hand-off to a running back, hides the ball against his body, and runs out wide of the outside men on the line of scrimmage. Usually used near the goal line, the bootleg was not a play the Monarchs made use of during the 1991 season.

Draw This is running play that starts off looking like a pass. The quarterback drops back and draws in the defensive linemen. He belatedly hands-off to a running back who takes advantage of the gaps left by the defenders and the fact that the defensive secondary has dropped back to await a pass. An often-used play in 1991 by the Monarchs, it brought them their first ever touchdown when David Smith ran in from 28 yards against Frankfurt.

Misdirection In a misdirection play, the running backs start moving in one direction before cutting back the other way, freezing and confusing the defensive linemen and taking advantage of any linebackers who have over-committed themselves. Monarchs running back Jeff Alexander scored several of his touchdowns with this move last season.

Play-action This is particularly effective when the defense is expecting a running play. The quarterback fakes a hand-off to the running back and then, with the defense committed, looks for an open receiver.

Sweep In a sweep, instead of rushing up the middle of the field, the running back runs to the outside, with offensive linemen leading the way for him. The running back must be quick enough to outrun the defense so that he can turn the corner and head upfield, but he must not overrun his blockers.

Screen pass On a screen pass, the quarterback fakes a hand-off and then throws a flat pass to his running back, who is waiting behind the line of scrimmage with a wall of blockers forming in front of him ready to escort him upfield. The Monarchs, with running back Judd Garrett, used this play a lot in 1991, including a 41-yard touchdown against Montreal.

INDEX